The Green Home

A *Sunset* Design Guide

by Bridget Biscotti Bradley and the editors of Sunset Books

Contents

Living green may seem difficult, expensive, and out of reach. But when you break it down into simple solutions for each room of the house, you'll see that it's really not. Every home can be made more energy and water efficient, we can all strive to reuse or recycle building materials and furnishings, and keeping indoor air quality healthful is easy when you know what the culprits are. This book will show you that green living is built on commonsense practices, smart home construction, and an awareness of how and where things are made. Making better choices will benefit the health of your family and the planet, and you'll save money in the end.

Throughout the book, you'll find straightforward advice on a variety of subjects from our panel of experts. Their collective experience in green building is enormous and we are honored to have their participation.

26

68

104

122

144

©2010 by Sunset Publishing Corporation
80 Willow Road, Menlo Park, CA 94025

ISBN-13: 978-0-376-01351-4
ISBN-10: 0-376-01351-6
Library of Congress Control
Number: 2008942795

10 9 8 7 6 5 4 3 2 1
First Printing January 2010
Printed in the United States of America

OXMOOR HOUSE, INC.
VP, Publishing Director: Jim Childs
Editorial Director: Susan Payne Dobbs
Brand Manager: Fonda Hitchcock
Managing Editor: L. Amanda Owens
Project Editors: Emily Chappell, Diane Rose

The Green Home: A Sunset Design Guide
CONTRIBUTORS
Author: Bridget Biscotti Bradley
Managing Editor: Bob Doyle
Photo Editor: Cynthia Del Fava
Copy Editor: John Edmonds
Page Production: Precision Graphics
Principal Photographer: Michele Lee Willson
Principal Photo Stylist: Laura Del Fava
Prepress Coordinator: Eligio Hernández
Proofreader: Denise Griffiths
Interns: Natalie Heard, Allison Sperando
Indexer: Marjorie Joy
Series Designer: Vasken Guiragossian

To order additional publications,
call 1-800-765-6400

For more books to enrich your life,
visit oxmoorhouse.com

Visit Sunset online at sunset.com

For the most comprehensive selection of
Sunset books, visit sunsetbooks.com

For more exciting home and garden ideas,
visit myhomeideas.com

Cover: Photography by Tim Story; design by
Linda Bouchard, Tracy Sunrize Johnson.
See credits for more information.

Design Panel

The following design
and building professionals
from across the United States
share their words of wisdom
throughout this book.

Eric Corey Freed
ARCHITECT

Eric Corey Freed is principal of organicARCHITECT,
an architecture and consulting firm in San Francisco.
He has nearly 20 years of experience in green
building. Eric teaches in the sustainable-design
program he developed at the Academy of Art
University and the University of California Berkeley
Extension. He sits on the boards of Architects,
Designers & Planners for Social Responsibility
(ADPSR), Green Home Guide, and West Coast
Green, as well as on the advisory boards of nearly a
dozen other organizations. San Francisco magazine
named organicARCHITECT the Best Green Architect
in 2005 and Best Visionary in 2007. Eric lectures
around the country at dozens of conferences each
year, and his work has been featured in Dwell,
Metropolis, Town & Country, Natural Home, and
Newsweek. He has appeared on television's HGTV,
Sundance Channel, and PBS.
www.organicarchitect.com

Paula Baker-Laporte
ARCHITECT

Paula Baker-Laporte graduated from the University
of Toronto's School of Architecture in 1978 and
from the International Institute of Bau-Biologie and
Ecology in 1995. In 2007, she was elected to the
College of Fellows of the American Institute of
Architects. She has headed a wide-ranging
architectural practice based in Santa Fe, New
Mexico, since 1986. Paula has dedicated her
practice to environmentally sound and health-
enhancing architecture. Her firm specializes in
healthful and natural design, as well as design and
consultation for people with chemical sensitivities.
Natural Home magazine selected her as one of
America's top 10 green architects in 2005.
www.econest.com
www.bakerlaporte.com

Iris Harrell
CONTRACTOR

Iris Harrell founded the design-build firm Harrell
Remodeling in 1985. She is a regularly invited
speaker at the National Association of Homebuild-
ers and the National Association of the Remodeling
Industry (NARI), where she encourages other
remodeling contractors to hire women for
nontraditional jobs. Iris's awards include the Fred
Case Remodeling Entrepreneur of the Year (one of
four nationally), the San Francisco Bay Area NARI
Marilyn Thurau Award, and Woman Contractor of
the Year in 1996 from Women Construction Owners
& Executives USA.
www.harrell-remodeling.com

Michelle Kaufmann
ARCHITECT

In 2002, Michelle Kaufmann founded Michelle Kaufmann Designs with the goal of making thoughtful, sustainable design accessible to everyone. A leader in the green design community, Michelle was dubbed the Henry Ford of green homes by *Sierra Club* magazine in 2007. Her work is widely published and has been showcased in a number of museums. Her company has won several awards for its work, including *Residential Architect* magazine's Top Firm in 2008.
www.mkd-arc.com

Matt Elliott
ARCHITECT

Matt Elliott received a bachelor's degree in architectural studies from the University of Illinois and a master's degree in architecture from the University of Pennsylvania. After graduating, he worked on residential, commercial, and institutional projects in the United States and abroad, and then started his firm in Maine in 1993. Elliott Elliott Norelius Architecture specializes in custom residential and small institutional projects in the Northeast. The firm sees good architecture as integrally addressing green issues, starting with the site right down to the smallest detail.
www.eena.com

Kelly LaPlante
INTERIOR DESIGNER

Kelly LaPlante has been demonstrating for more than a decade that green is a standard, not a style. Her projects include residences, hotels, and restaurants around the globe, as well as *jak*, her studio collection of eco-friendly furniture with designer James Saavedra. She has appeared on many television programs, including Discovery Home Channel's *Greenovate* and Sundance Channel's *Big Ideas for a Small Planet*.
www.kellylaplante.com

Jason Lear
CONTRACTOR

Jason Lear specializes in building extremely energy-efficient houses using nothing fancy at all. In 2007 his firm, Batt + Lear, was the only company in Seattle to certify a 5-Star Built Green remodel. In 2008, it won the Built Green Hammer Award, given by the Master Builders' Association. Jason received a bachelor's degree in architecture and international studies from Yale University.
www.battandlear.com

Peter Pfeiffer
ARCHITECT

Peter Pfeiffer is an architect and building scientist who was named a fellow of the American Institute of Architects for his achievements in developing practical yet high-performance green-building strategies. He is a principal of Barley & Pfeiffer Architects in Austin, Texas, whose work has been featured in the *Washington Post,* the *New York Times,* and *Better Homes & Gardens*. The company has also been featured on NPR and HGTV. In 2006, *Residential Architect* magazine cited Peter as one of the 10 most influential architects of the past decade.
www.barleypfeiffer.com

Chapter 1

Getting Started

Your desire for a healthier, more sustainably built, energy-efficient home has brought you to this book, and we are here to guide you toward that goal. We'll walk you through each room of the house, discussing material choices and other options for healthy living, but first let's talk about what makes a home green. It doesn't have to be a prefabricated house or one that scores high on one of the major green home rating scales. It doesn't even have to be new. You can improve upon the efficiency and indoor air quality of any home once you know what to look for. Green building is simply smart building, resulting in homes that are long lasting and affordable. This chapter will start you thinking along those lines.

What Is Green Living?

Deep overhangs on the south side of the house protect windows from too much direct sun, so the homeowner won't turn on the air conditioner as much, if at all.

This book focuses on living green—a state of awareness about your surroundings and how they affect your family's health and the health of the planet. According to the U.S. Green Building Council, buildings in the United States account for 72 percent of the nation's electricity consumption, 39 percent of energy use, 38 percent of all carbon dioxide emissions, and 14 percent of potable-water consumption. Therefore, each of us has a role to play as we consider how energy efficient and sustainable our homes should be. Not everyone is in the market to build a new house, but that doesn't mean you can't make positive changes to the one you have. Whether you're thinking of painting a few rooms, embarking on a full kitchen remodel, decorating a nursery, buying some new furniture, or relandscaping, this book suggests the most eco-friendly way to go.

Energy Efficiency

A green home is first and foremost energy efficient. It may not be glamorous, but making sure that your house is well insulated and that your fixtures and appliances aren't wasting water should be top concerns. The world is quickly running out of potable water, and in years to come, water will almost certainly be scarcer and more expensive. Even now,

some brands of bottled water cost more than an equivalent amount of oil. Do your part to conserve by switching out water-guzzling toilets, washing machines, and dishwashers.

Will you be able to afford your home in 10 or 20 years? You're probably paying more than ever to heat and cool your house, and with the instability of oil and electricity prices, there's every likelihood that the situation will eventually grow worse. Plan ahead by making sure that your home is fully insulated, that you have energy-efficient windows, and that your hot-water pipes are insulated. If it makes sense in your region and for the amount you spend on electricity, install solar panels. If you're building a new house, spend time analyzing the site so you can take advantage of the sun's patterns to help heat and cool your home naturally. We'll explore these issues in later chapters.

TOP LEFT Exchange old showerheads for those that use no more than 1.6 gallons of water per minute.

TOP RIGHT Old homes can be made more energy efficient. This 1920s farmhouse now features solar panels and a rainwater-collection system.

ABOVE A home with plenty of natural light will have lower electric bills than one that relies on electric lights during the day.

CONTRACTOR
JASON LEAR ON

What Makes the Difference

There is no one silver bullet that makes a house green. Everything contributes to it, including what kind of sheathing you choose, where you put your pipes and ducts, and even how you apply the caulk at every stage of construction. That's where a good builder comes in. Don't depend on the building code to make sure the house is being constructed in an energy-efficient way. The benefits of having a builder who slows down and does things carefully with energy efficiency in mind will make the difference between a house with high heating bills and one that is closer to self-sufficient."

TOP LEFT A tiny bathroom feels bigger with a large skylight. The tub is equipped with a handheld showerhead for a seated bather or a parent who needs to clean a small child.

BOTTOM LEFT In this quilting room, the Murphy bed can be hidden inside a cabinet when not needed.

ARCHITECT
PETER PFEIFFER ON

Universal Design

There are ways in which universal design collides with the green-building movement. Green houses should have small footprints, but if you add square footage by building wider doorways or build a one-story house for accessibility when a two-story home would consume less energy, the two goals become mutually exclusive. Strike a balance between universal-design features and what will be cheaper to own and operate."

Universal Design

Universal design is a way of building houses and commercial spaces to be accessible to everyone, no matter how short or tall, young or old, physically able or disabled a person may be. Building green means building for the long term, so everything in a house should be as easy for elderly people to use as it is for a young family. Make sure there are ramps instead of, or in addition to, stairs at all entrances. Include sections of kitchen cabinets that are lower and higher than the standard heights so that work surfaces are comfortable for short and tall people to use. Put appliances where you can reach them without stooping down or standing on a step stool. Use hands-free or easy-to-grip faucets, and put levers instead of knobs on doors so that people with reduced hand strength can operate them. Also make sure there's ample lighting for reading and task work.

While it's not always possible when you're remodeling, if you're building a new house, consider making all doorways wide enough for a wheelchair and allow for appropriate turning radiuses in the bathrooms and kitchen. Contractor Iris Harrell encourages her clients to think ahead on this issue. "Even if you can't imagine yourself needing these features, what if your mother or a friend can't come visit you because of the stairs leading to your home? Some builders say that you should incorporate universal-design features only if you plan to live in the house when you're elderly, but even if you don't, another family may someday need those features, or a guest to your home may need them," Harrell says.

Smaller Is Better

To live within your means has always been good advice, and today that includes living in a home that's sized for you and that you can afford to heat and cool. It takes a lot of electricity, gas, and water to power large houses, so if you don't need all the space you have, consider moving to a place with a smaller footprint to save energy in the long run. And if you are building a new house, size it appropriately. Harrell advises her clients to create multipurpose rooms rather than more rooms with specific purposes. "Think about how many times a year you'll need a guest room versus needing a studio or an art room. Incorporating Murphy beds makes any room a guest room when needed, but the bed is usually hidden away so the space can be used for other daily purposes," she says.

Foot pedals installed at the toe-kick operate this wall-mounted faucet, making it easier for people with reduced hand strength to use.

What Makes a Product Green?

With most manufacturers trying to convince you that their products are eco-friendly, it's becoming tough to determine which ones really are the best products and materials for your health and the environment. But once you understand the following terms, you'll be able to use common sense to figure out whether companies are telling the truth or not.

RAPIDLY RENEWABLE RESOURCES are materials that regenerate quickly in nature. Bamboo is a renewable resource because stalks grow to maturity in five to seven years, plus they require no pesticides and little water to grow. Today bamboo is used for flooring, cabinets, countertops, and even clothes and towels. Who knew those leafy stalks could be turned into incredibly soft, absorbent, and fast-drying fabric? Renewable materials are also biodegradable and are produced from agricultural crops, so they don't take energy other than the sun to grow (although some require significant energy to manufacture, which is another factor to consider). Cork, wheatboard, organic cotton, and wool are other examples of renewable materials.

RECYCLED AND SALVAGED MATERIALS are being used in carpets, countertops, lighting fixtures, and more. Anytime

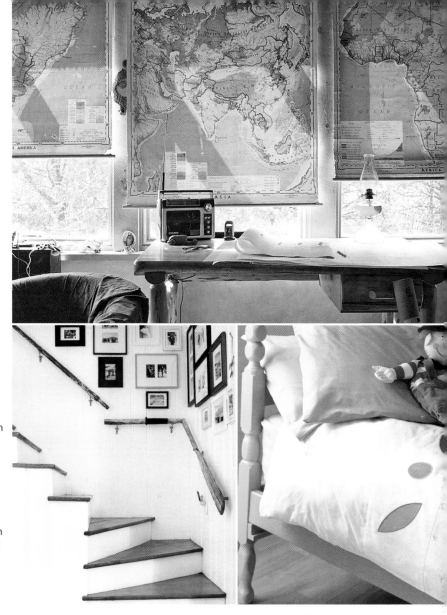

LEFT This dual-purpose kitchen and workspace was created with reclaimed wood, a salvaged soapstone sink, string lights, and secondhand furniture.

TOP These old pull-down maps now serve as unique window coverings.

RIGHT Wooden boat oars make great stair rails.

FAR RIGHT Pure cotton bedding and solid-wood furniture are renewable, sustainable materials that can be recycled at the end of their useful life. At worst, they are completely biodegradable.

you use something that would have otherwise ended up in a landfill, it's a good thing. Reusing what already exists is almost always better for the environment than making something from virgin materials, whether it means buying a table at a garage sale, gathering waste from one manufacturing process to use as an ingredient in something else, or re-milling beams from a torn-down building into tongue-and-groove flooring. Products that incorporate post-consumer recycled content (such as used bottles) are generally considered more eco-friendly than those incorporating pre-consumer recycled content (such as manufacturing waste).

CONTRACTOR
JASON LEAR ON THE

Benefits of Salvage

Most of the time, a homeowner wants to be involved in the project in some way, either to defray costs or to lend a little sweat equity. I encourage my clients to spend time searching online and at local salvage yards for something they can reuse, whether it's an old door, insulation that hasn't been compressed or gotten wet, or old studs made of far sturdier stock than what you can buy new to frame a wall. Sometimes you have to act quickly and you may not even be sure you can use your finds, but if you have a place to store them during the building process, the payback can be huge both in pride and your bottom line."

LOW- OR NO-VOC PRODUCTS are those that emit little to no volatile organic compounds (VOCs). Because so many products in our homes release VOCs over time—including furniture made of plywood or particleboard, vinyl shower curtains, mattresses and upholstery treated with fire or stain retardants, and carpeting—the air quality inside our homes is often much worse than it is outdoors. According to the American Lung Association, VOCs can cause eye and skin irritation, breathing problems, headaches and nausea, muscle weakness, and liver and kidney damage. People with chemical sensitivity often can't live comfortably in spaces with even minimal amounts of VOCs, while others aren't as noticeably affected. These toxins affect mostly children, the elderly, and people with weakened immune systems, but the combination of all of these chemicals in our homes may be a factor in the development of cancer and other serious illnesses.

In addition to being dangerous inside your home, VOCs eventually migrate outdoors, where they mix with other substances in the air and turn into ozone, which is a component of smog. So buying low- or no-VOC materials is important not just for your own health but for the health of the planet.

Federal and state legislation now regulates the amount of VOCs contained in coatings such as paint and stain. Laws vary by state, but generally manufacturers must limit the VOCs in their finishes to 350 grams per liter. For a product to be considered low-VOC, it must generally contain no more than 50 grams per liter. VOCs in other products, such as furniture and mattresses, are not regulated, which is why it's important to look for products that have other environmental certifications, such as Greenguard (see page 17).

OPPOSITE PAGE
Reclaimed bricks, solid-wood furniture made locally, and breathable plaster walls are all sustainable choices.

TOP LEFT Hardwood flooring can be refinished, making it a long-lasting flooring choice. The reclaimed table and library drawer unit are well-made and will likely be in use for decades.

TOP RIGHT Incorporating trees and stones that already exist on your property into the design of the house makes the home feel more connected to the site. And the building materials certainly didn't have to travel far to get there.

BOTTOM No-VOC paint doesn't look any different on your walls, but it's much better for your indoor air quality and the environment.

LOCALLY PRODUCED PRODUCTS, just like locally grown food, are eco-friendly because they didn't have to travel far to get to you, resulting in fewer carbon emissions along the way. A marble countertop from China that travels by truck and boat to get to your door takes a lot more gas and energy than ceramic tiles made locally, for example.

DURABILITY is not a green feature you hear much about, but it stands to reason that buying well-made furnishings that will last a lifetime is more eco-friendly than buying something less well-made that will wear out or fall apart and end up in the trash. Yes, you will pay more for well-made products, but think of the money you'll save over time when you don't have to buy the same thing every 5 or 10 years. Similarly, low-maintenance items are often considered eco-friendly because you won't have to paint or stain them as frequently, meaning they will have less of an environmental impact over time.

The cabinets in this bright and cheerful small kitchen are covered in a sustainably harvested vertical-grain white fir veneer. Some of the door faces are stained a bright red, and all of the wood is protected with a low-VOC sealant.

ENERGY-SAVING PRODUCTS are of course green, even if they are made with materials that are not. For example, high-performance windows made out of PVC vinyl are a green product because they make the building more energy efficient—even though they are made with a material that is unhealthful for the environment and people, both during its production and at the end of its life cycle. There are, however, a growing number of energy-saving products that are made with nontoxic and recyclable materials, such as recycled cotton denim insulation.

ENVIRONMENTAL CERTIFICATIONS can help you determine whether what you're buying was brought to you in a responsible way. For example, buying wood that is certified by the Forest Stewardship Council means that the wood harvesting was legal, that the forest wasn't clear-cut and old-growth trees weren't used, that the rights of indigenous communities and workers were respected, and that wildlife habitats were not negatively affected. While there are other certification bodies, only the FSC has the full support of the environmental community, including Greenpeace and the Sierra Club.

There are many other independent certifications for products ranging from household cleaners to furniture to mattresses. Green Seal conducts scientific tests to ensure that eco-friendly products work as well as or better than others in their class, and the organization visits the manufacturing plant to ensure that the production process has little or no impact on the environment. Look for the Green Seal logo on paints, cleaners, and floor-care products.

Greenguard tests products for the amount of chemical and particle emissions they release, and certifies that they are healthful for your indoor air quality. It tests construction products such as adhesives and insulation; interior furnishings, including electronic

ARCHITECT
MATT ELLIOTT ON

Getting to Know Your Suppliers

Certification programs like FSC are great for home-owners sourcing their own materials and for professionals in areas where lumber isn't sourced. Here in Maine, there are a lot of lumber mills. Most aren't certified but they are practicing sustainable harvesting and can show me exactly where the wood is coming from. In areas like this, with a rich history of milling, you can learn more about lumber talking to a guy at the mill than you can after 10 years as an architect."

TOP Surround yourself with natural materials such as cotton, wool, and wood rather than polyester and vinyl.

ABOVE LEFT Green Seal–certified Yolo Colorhouse paint is VOC-free, making it among the healthiest products you can put on your walls.

ABOVE RIGHT Made from eucalyptus trees grown on sustainable South American plantations, this kitchen island is an eco-friendly choice because the wood is harvested faster than other types of hardwood.

equipment and wooden furniture; and finishing materials such as floor, wall, and window coverings.

Cradle to Cradle certification looks at the complete life cycle of a product and all of its ingredients. Products certified by Cradle to Cradle will either biodegrade and restore the soil or be fully recycled into high-quality materials for new products, eliminating the concept of waste. The type and quality of energy required to make a product, the water quantity and quality involved, and the manufacturer's social responsibility are also considered in the certification process.

Balancing the Issues

It can sometimes be daunting to remember all of the factors that make a product eco-friendly and balance those issues with your needs and budget, the style of your house, and the health of your family and the environment. If the most important thing to you is indoor air quality, then you might select a product that was manufactured far away or that does not incorporate any recycled materials, simply because it uses no-VOC finishes. If carbon emissions are what you're most concerned about, you may choose a product made locally, even though it isn't low-maintenance and will require the application of chemical finishes to refresh it every few years. There are very few products that meet every single criterion discussed on the previous pages. To help you weigh the factors, ask the following questions about the product you're considering:

- Where did the product come from?
- How many miles did it travel to get to you?
- What mode of transportation was used?
- What is the product made of?
- Are any recycled materials incorporated?
- Did it take a great deal of energy to produce this product?
- Are there any toxic chemicals in it that will offgas in your home?
- Was it manufactured in a way that doesn't harm the environment or workers' health?
- How long will this product last, and when it is no longer usable, will it be biodegradable?

LEFT Vetrazzo countertops are made in Northern California with pre- and post-consumer recycled glass and concrete. If you live in that area, you'd be hard-pressed to find a more eco-friendly countertop option.

LEFT This kitchen features energy-efficient lighting and appliances, no-VOC paint, and FSC-certified hardwood floors, though the marble was flown in from Italy. On the whole, good decisions were made.

TOP RIGHT Resurfacing a vintage tub requires high-VOC chemicals, but once the process is done, the tub can continue its useful life for another 20 to 30 years rather than sitting in a landfill. So overall, it is a green choice.

RIGHT This farmhouse sink is made of recycled aluminum. It's extremely durable, and the brushed finish makes it easy to keep clean.

ARCHITECT
ERIC COREY FREED ON

Indoor Air Quality

My clients often seem to go through the five stages of grief in regard to indoor air quality—something I give primary importance to when I'm designing homes. First I tell them that most homes contain toxins and I'm met with denial. 'Well, I feel fine,' they'll say. Then I back that statement up with facts and the person gets angry. 'Why isn't there a government agency doing something about this?' they'll demand. Then comes bargaining. 'I bought this at Ikea, and I hear it's quite green,' they'll offer. Then I show proof again and they get depressed about it, until finally there's acceptance. It can be very disheartening to look around your existing home and see the formaldehyde and the vinyl and the VOCs, but it's empowering to know what we can do about it. Today we always have a healthful green product to use, whereas 15 years ago, we didn't."

Indoor Air Quality

Situated in a breezeway, this living room has breathtaking views of the garden, in addition to plenty of sunlight and fresh air.

Given the rapidly increasing rates of people with asthma, allergies, learning disorders, and attention-deficit disorder, scientists are looking to our homes for answers. Studies have shown that our bodies carry around chemicals that people were not exposed to a generation ago. Of the approximately 80,000 chemicals on the market today, fewer than 10 percent have been tested for their effect on humans; and the health consequences of the combination of all the chemicals we surround ourselves with is largely unknown. Because of the synthetic materials most people now live with, the air inside a house is likely to be two to five times as toxic as outdoor air, and that number can spike to 100 right after a product that emits high levels of VOCs has been used, such as common household cleaners or oil-based paint.

Removing the Offenders

How can you improve these statistics? First, as much as possible, remove products that are offgasing in your home. Prime suspects are bottles of adhesives, paints and finishes, and cleaning supplies; carpet; conventional upholstered furniture and mattresses made with petrochemical-based foam and treated with flame retardants; and conventional engineered wood. Sometimes it doesn't make sense to remove every possible offender—ripping out functioning kitchen cabinets that were painted with oil-based enamel is not an eco-friendly choice. A complete removal is necessary only for people who are chemically sensitive or have other severe breathing or immune diseases.

Start with the easy changes that everyone will benefit from. For example, all adhesives and paints should be stored away from living spaces, even if the lids are on tight. If you have any products that you no longer use and don't need to store, dispose of them in an environmentally responsible way. Begin using cleaning products that are better for your indoor air quality (see "Cleaning" at right). And then the next time you do need to buy something

for the house, be it flooring or a new chair, consider what it's made of and whether it will offgas before making the purchase.

Keeping Toxins Out

During a remodel, be most careful to keep toxins from filtering through the house, as this is when many harmful gases and particulates can be released. Make sure all vents are sealed so dust and fumes won't migrate from room to room. Buy low- or no-VOC building and finish materials whenever possible. When it's not possible, let high-VOC products offgas somewhere else before being moved into your home. Also, hire only contractors who sign on to this concept and who agree to keep toxic materials out of your house. See chapter 7 for more information.

Ventilation Is Key

Use a combination of natural and mechanical ventilation to ensure that stale air won't stagnate in your home. Also invest in a whole-house air filter for your furnace to trap particulates, dust, and dander. Bringing outside air into the house is usually a good way to clean it out, but in some areas where there is a lot of humidity, allowing outdoor air to come inside can lead to problems with dust mites and mold. See chapter 3 for more information on ventilation.

If you have an attached garage, make sure the door leading to your house is well-sealed. Otherwise, fumes from stored paints, fertilizer, insecticides, and your car can still get in your home. For this reason, architect Peter Pfeiffer encourages clients to build houses with detached garages. "If you already have an attached garage, use foam insulation to isolate the air in the garage and keep it from migrating to the house or the attic. Then make sure there are plenty of vents in the garage itself. I advise clients to install an exhaust fan that automatically turns on every time the garage door opens," Pfeiffer says.

Cleaning

One of the easiest and best ways to start living green today is to banish air-polluting cleaning products from your home. If you get a headache

or your eyes start to water every time you clean the bathroom, your body is telling you something. Most conventional cleaners are made from petroleum products and may contain fragrances and other solvents that are suspected hormone disrupters and don't biodegrade. They can also cause rashes, allergic reactions, and difficulty in breathing.

We tend to overclean our homes, using antibacterial products and bleach, when these types of products aren't really needed for successful cleaning. Antibacterial cleaners don't let our immune systems function in a healthy way and actually promote the growth of resistant strains of bacteria. Chlorine bleach is a common ingredient in tile and toilet-bowl cleaners, but you're sending toxins that harm reproductive and neurological systems down the drain and breathing them in while you work. Not to mention that bleach can be fatal if swallowed and creates a toxic chlorine gas when mixed with any product containing ammonia.

If you must use bleach, look for fragrance-free nonchlorine bleach that's at least less harmful to our water supplies.

While there are more choices than ever for cleaning products that won't negatively affect your indoor air quality, don't be fooled by misleading marketing. Products labeled "natural" are not necessarily nontoxic. Read the labels and look for organic or vegetable-based ingredients that are fragrance-free or contain natural essential oils for fragrance. You should be able to pronounce and even recognize the ingredients. If you can't, keep looking. These rules apply to air fresheners, detergents, and metal polishes too.

Greening your cleaning routine can also save you some cash. Instead of buying name-brand nontoxic home cleaners, you can make your own. There are lots of websites that tell you how, but basically you can clean most anything with water, baking soda, vinegar, lemon juice, and borax.

FAR LEFT Take wool blankets and throw pillows outside at least a couple of times a year to let them air out and benefit from the natural whitening and sanitizing power of sunlight.

ABOVE LEFT Make your house a shoe-free zone to keep out dust, dander, and chemicals you've picked up from the ground outside. This will make the house much easier to keep clean.

ABOVE Clean your silver with biodegradable, nontoxic products. Or fill an aluminum pan with 1 teaspoon of baking soda and 1 teaspoon of salt per cup of boiling water and place your silver in the hot water. The tarnish on the silver will be pulled off and deposited onto the aluminum. You can also do this in a glass bowl covered with aluminum foil.

ABOVE RIGHT There are many nontoxic cleaners and detergents on the market today. Or you can save money and make your own cleaning supplies with ingredients you probably already have in your kitchen cupboards.

INTERIOR DESIGNER KELLY LAPLANTE ON

Avoiding Mothballs

Remember that smell of mothballs in your grandmother's attic? Now we know that the active ingredient in mothballs is a pesticide that the Environmental Protection Agency considers a possible carcinogen linked to cataracts and liver and neurological damage. Instead, use cedar closets, chests, or shavings near your valuable wool sweaters. Or make up a batch of your own herbal moth repellant using cloves, rosemary, lavender, eucalyptus, cinnamon sticks, bay leaves, or a combination of these. It will work just as well and be much better for your indoor air quality."

Green Rating Systems

One of the most highly rated GreenPoint homes in California to date, this Craftsman-style house features solar panels, a geothermal heat pump, a 10,000-gallon rainwater-collection system, FSC-certified Douglas fir and cherry cabinets, no-VOC paint, salvaged walnut flooring, and recycled-glass countertops.

So how green is your house? There are plenty of green rating systems that will answer that question for you. If you're building a new house, strive to make it as eco-friendly as it can be. Consider building it using the guidelines of one or more of the organizations that follow, and have it rated when it's done. There could be a substantial tax break in it for you. Even if you're just remodeling, these resources will point you in the right direction.

LEED stands for Leadership in Energy and Environmental Design. It's an independent certification program that rates buildings in five key areas: sustainable site development, water savings, energy efficiency, materials selection, and indoor environmental quality. There are different criteria for different types of buildings, from new construction to existing schools, retail spaces, and homes. Projects must meet certain prerequisites to be candidates for LEED certification. It is most helpful to have a LEED-certified consultant or project manager to guide you through this process. Buildings that earn certification have lower operating costs, reduce waste, conserve energy and water, are healthier and safer for occupants, and, in many cities, qualify for tax rebates, zoning allowances, and other financial incentives.

THE HERS INDEX, or Home Energy Rating System, assesses whether a home meets the standards of Energy Star for Homes, a program run by the Environmental Protection Agency. The idea is to rate homes based only on how much energy they use—the goal being a net-zero-energy home, of which there are currently very few.

THE NATIONAL GREEN BUILDING PROGRAM, developed by the National Association of Home Builders, allows contractors to certify that their new homes are sustainably designed and built.

REGIONAL RATING SYSTEMS are popping up all over the country. In California, there's GreenPoint Rated, a program that scores homes using the same criteria for energy efficiency, resource conservation, indoor air quality, water conservation, and community so that consumers can compare homes on a level playing field.

The Next Generation of Green Rating Systems

Contractor Jason Lear has been participating in the rewriting of one of his local rating systems, Seattle's Built Green checklist. "Ours is really an educational program," Lear explains. "In the end, our highest goal is to bring more people to green building, and we are achieving that." But he feels that soon clients will need to expect their contractors to use green building principles as standard practice, rather than building green just to meet the expectations of a rating system. Otherwise, he says, things may not progress in the way they need to.

Lear believes builders need to focus on the performance of buildings rather than on checking items off a list. "There are some flaws with green rating systems. I believe that if you put a house that is newly certified under one program or another to the test, you might find that it isn't performing any better than a noncertified equivalent," he says. "Cities like Portland and Seattle have begun to adopt such programs as policies, giving those centers of government the opportunity to stand up and declare their intentions to be more responsible and make better buildings—to say, if our buildings aren't actually saving energy, then we've missed the mark. And the only way to know that is if we gather the data, test as we build, and make sure we really are building high-performance buildings and not just using green materials that could be installed incorrectly."

Chapter 2

Living Spaces

The materials you surround yourself with—from flooring and wall coverings to furniture and accessories—have a great impact on the health of your home. This chapter walks you through all of the choices and steers you toward the most eco-friendly options in each category. A common misconception is that to have a green home, you must choose finish materials that are unusual or have a certain "au naturel" style. This is far from true. What building materials and furnishings are made of, where they come from, and how they are finished are what counts. The style is completely up to you.

Flooring

Cork flooring is warm and resilient, and it now comes prefinished for easier maintenance.

There are so many factors to consider when you are choosing a new floor. Will it be exposed to moisture or heavy traffic, or be used to exercise or play on? Will the flooring material you want work over radiant heat, a concrete slab, or an existing material that would be difficult or dangerous to remove? Beyond the issues related to the anticipated level of use, location, and installation, there are styles and aesthetics to consider. Luckily, many eco-friendly flooring options are available today, so finding one that you like the look of and that serves your purposes should be easy.

Even if money is tight, avoid settling on something you think of as a short-term solution. Buying high-quality, long-lasting building materials will save you money in the long run and is better for the environment as well.

LEFT Wood flooring is a sustainable option as it can be refinished many times and then recycled when no longer needed as a floor.

TOP RIGHT Slate floor tiles absorb the heat from the fire and slowly release it through the day, reducing the need for supplemental heating systems.

BOTTOM RIGHT Wool area rugs can make a living room feel homier.

Wood

Natural wood is beautiful and long lasting, plus there are wood species and colors that will work with every style of home. And these days, you don't have to sacrifice your environmental values to have hardwood floors. All of the most popular types, including oak, cherry, and walnut—and even tropical woods such as Brazilian cherry and Patagonian rosewood—are now available from sustainable and environmentally certified forests. But the only way to know for sure that you're buying eco-friendly wood flooring is to see the Forest Stewardship Council label (see page 17 for more information on the FSC). This is particularly important because deforestation and the burning of tropical forests is one of the main causes of global warming. Spending your money on FSC-certified products will encourage more landowners to conduct business in a sustainable way, eventually reducing the amount of carbon dioxide in the atmosphere.

Many wood-flooring manufacturers use green words like "sustainable," "managed," and "certified," but the terms alone don't mean much. There are some forest-certification systems that have weak environmental protections and allow large-scale clearing of old-growth trees. So you have to be diligent about the wood's FSC certification. Get proof that the actual wood you receive is FSC-certified, not just that you're buying the wood from a company that has FSC certification. The packaging should be labeled as such if the wood is FSC-certified.

You have a choice of solid or engineered wood flooring, available either unfinished or with stain and sealant already applied. Prefinished wood flooring will cost more per square foot than unfinished planks, but you'll find it often turns out to be less expensive once you factor in the additional installation cost to sand, stain, and seal the floor, plus the inconvenience of vacating the house for one or more weeks while the floor is being worked on. Prefinished wood flooring is also better for your indoor air quality: Even if you use low-VOC stains and sealants on unfinished flooring, there will be some offgassing in your home, not to mention a large amount of sanding dust. Look for prefinished flooring that uses low- or no-VOC stains and sealants, and engineered flooring that contains formaldehyde-free adhesives. A high-quality engineered floor also has enough of a wear layer on top to withstand at least two rounds of refinishing, should that be necessary down the line.

OPPOSITE PAGE Wood is equally at home in grand and quaint spaces. Shown here is EcoTimber's FSC-certified, formaldehyde-free, prefinished White Tigerwood engineered wood flooring.

TOP LEFT Unstained white oak has a natural look that goes well with icy blue walls.

TOP RIGHT Nothing beats the depth and pattern of wood floors.

RIGHT Hand-scraped hickory prefinished with no-VOC stain and sealant provides a rustic look for less money than reclaimed wood that needs to be finished after installation.

ARCHITECT
PETER PFEIFFER ON

Installing Wood Floors

I like to install hardwood flooring on sleepers—wood planks that lift the finished flooring off the subfloor—to allow for air circulation and a bit of give. This is slightly more expensive, and it's tough to do in a remodel, but it will feel much more comfortable underfoot than wood glued onto a concrete subfloor. As people age, they tend to feel it in their legs and back when they are walking on hard materials."

TOP Knots, splits, and old nail holes give some types of reclaimed-wood flooring character, making it a great choice for homes that will take some abuse from kids and pets.

BOTTOM LEFT Expect a range of tones when you purchase reclaimed-wood flooring.

BOTTOM RIGHT Reclaimed wood was re-milled into this smooth and even wide-plank flooring.

Some people may assume that reclaimed-wood flooring looks rustic, but that's not always the case. There are varieties that have old nail holes and splits, but there are also choices that look clean and new. If you want to make reclaimed wood look its age, ask your installer to hand-scrape it for a more undulating surface.

CONTRACTOR
IRIS HARRELL ON

Durability of Wood Floors

If you have a wood floor already, it's always the greener choice to refinish it rather than to rip it out in favor of another type of flooring, especially if you also use no- or low-VOC stains and sealants. Some people get nervous about having a wood floor in the kitchen, but lots of people are doing it now so that the floor can flow into an adjoining great room. There's no reason a wood floor can't perform well in a kitchen, unless you have large dogs or kids riding through on skateboards. If you're still worried, stain the wood a dark color so that dirty joint lines won't be as noticeable."

Reclaimed Wood

Reclaimed-wood flooring is usually made of wood salvaged from old buildings or bridges, or from logs found in rivers and lakes. Because the wood comes in all sizes and varying degrees of distress, it's usually re-milled into tongue-and-groove planks. Sometimes you can find existing flooring that has been carefully salvaged from an old building, and the history and patina of the old floor can simply be transferred to your house. Try to find reclaimed wood from sources as close to where you live as possible, as it takes a lot of energy to locate, re-mill, and ship it across the country.

If you already have a hardwood floor in one part of an old home and want to extend it to other rooms, reclaimed wood may be a better visual match than new wood. Reclaimed wood is also more stable than new wood, meaning it expands and contracts less over time.

Wood flooring salvaged from old chicken coops adds to the character of this 1860s home.

TOP The bamboo stalks in this Plyboo floor were placed end-up before being pressed into planks, making the floor appear almost out of focus.

BOTTOM Natural-colored bamboo is a pale yellow, shown here coordinated with bamboo veneer on kitchen cabinets.

Bamboo

How many times have you heard someone talk about an eco-friendly home and list bamboo flooring as the main feature? Bamboo is considered synonymous with green design, but its environmental impact is a mixed picture.

Bamboo requires no pesticides or chemical fertilizers to grow, and it reaches maturity in about five years. Wood of comparable hardness can take 50 or more years to mature. Because of this, bamboo is a sustainable choice, but that is only one factor to consider. Bamboo is grown mostly in forests and on plantations in Asia, so it often travels a long way to its end destination. It also takes a lot of energy to turn bamboo stalks into flooring planks, and some manufacturers use high-VOC resins and finishes, which negate other green features.

There are three choices for bamboo flooring: solid, which is made of solid bamboo stalks that are pressed and glued together; engineered, which combines bamboo wear layers with fiberboard cores; and strand-woven, which consists of shredded bamboo stalks that are pressed and glued together.

When strips of bamboo are glued so that the wider side of the stalk faces up, it's referred to as horizontal-grain bamboo. Flooring made of stalks glued together on their sides is called vertical-grain bamboo.

The natural color of bamboo is a light blond, but the strips can be carbonized, a process during which the natural sugars are caramelized until they turn a light amber color. Cooking the bamboo in this way results in flooring that is about 20 percent softer than natural-colored bamboo, but scratches and dents are better disguised in the darker color. Bamboo doesn't accept stain evenly, so most manufacturers offer only natural and amber colors. Strand-woven bamboo looks more like wood, and it is also much harder than regular bamboo because of the resin used to bind the shredded fibers.

Some people who installed bamboo years ago have been disappointed with the way it wears, citing circumstances in which the flooring has delaminated or been easily marred by scratches and dents. Horizontal- and vertical-grain bamboo rate about 1,200 on the Janka hardness scale (about the same as oak), an industrywide measure for comparing the hardness of all wood species. During the Janka test, a hard, round object is thrown at the wood and a number is generated based on the amount of impact needed to create a dent. Bamboo fibers don't react the same way as wood does to this kind of impact test. The bamboo fibers tend to bounce the round object out rather than accepting the impact by denting. So if bamboo and hardwood have identical Janka test ratings, the hardwood floor will actually wear better than the bamboo. With a Janka rating of 3,000, strand-woven bamboo is a better choice for homes with active children or large animals.

INTERIOR DESIGNER
KELLY LAPLANTE ON

Bamboo

Many clients initially choose bamboo because they think that's the 'look' of green, but we believe there is no such thing as a green style. They may believe they can't get eco-friendly wood floors, but once we explain FSC certification to them, many choose that route instead. It's true that bamboo is a sustainable product in the way it's grown, but you have to be careful, as many manufacturers add formaldehyde-based adhesives and toxic finishes, making the end result anything but eco-friendly. It must be purchased from a reputable company that doesn't savage wild bamboo forests or add ingredients that will negatively affect indoor air quality."

Strand-woven bamboo mimics the grain of hardwood, making it suitable in practically any style of home.

Cork

Soft and warm underfoot, cork is easy on your back, resists denting, absorbs sound, reduces heat transfer and vibrations, and is naturally insect-repellent. Cork flooring is usually made from post-industrial waste—the leftovers of the cork-stopper manufacturing process. The raw material comes from the bark of the cork oak tree, grown most commonly in Mediterranean regions, and can be harvested every nine years without harm to the living tree. Although the material itself is sustainable, the end product is eco-friendly only if you buy products without added formaldehyde that have been finished with no- or low-VOC sealants.

Available as glue-down tiles or sheets and as clickable floating planks, cork works for many applications. When cork flooring was installed in the 1950s and 1960s, it was not sold prefinished, so there are people who have bad memories of never being able to get it clean. Today you can get prefinished cork that wipes up as easily as other resilient floor coverings. It's a good idea to add another coat of sealant right after installing cork in a bathroom or kitchen so that any spills won't seep into gaps between the tiles.

Linoleum

In the early 1900s, linoleum was a popular, practical choice, but the midcentury emergence of vinyl as a cheaper and more durable option made linoleum seem old-fashioned. While vinyl is more resistant to moisture and

LEFT Linoleum is a healthful alternative to vinyl in the kitchen.

RIGHT Available in an ever-expanding array of patterns and colors, cork can make a bold design statement and is easy on your joints.

stains and comes in a wider range of colors and patterns, it is also one of the least eco-friendly flooring choices on the market. Vinyl flooring is made of polyvinyl chloride (PVC) and contains a dangerous chemical called dioxin, which is released into the air during manufacturing and also if the floor ever catches fire. Manufacturers claim that vinyl is a green product because it's long lasting (i.e., it will never decompose) and doesn't need to be resealed. But PVC is a hormone-disrupting carcinogen that is bad for the environment when it's made, as well as at the end of its life cycle.

Linoleum, on the other hand, is a completely natural material made of linseed oil, cork dust, wood flour, tree resins, ground limestone, and natural pigments. The manufacturing process and eventual disposal of linoleum do not involve any environmental toxins. Linoleum is available as tile or sheet flooring that can be glued down or installed as a floating floor without adhesive. Because the pattern and color aren't just printed on top, as with vinyl flooring, you can fill in scratches with shavings of a leftover tile mixed with wood glue. Although linseed oil is harmless, some people are annoyed by the smell, so you should give linoleum tiles a good whiff before installing them if you're very sensitive to smells. The scent will dissipate over time.

CONTRACTOR
JASON LEAR ON

Choosing Cork for Bathrooms and Kitchens

Installing cork in a bathroom is similar to installing wood in a bathroom: It's not the most water-resistant choice, but if you have good ventilation in the room and you don't leave standing water on the floor, it will do fine. In the kitchen, the renewability and beauty of cork, as well as the daily benefits on your back, may far outweigh the possibility that your dishwasher might one day leak when you're not home and cause the floor to warp."

Laminate

Laminate flooring can look like wood, tile, or stone. The main body of the flooring is typically tongue-and-groove high-density fiberboard that contains urea-formaldehyde binders. On top of that is either a printed image of wood grain or a thin piece of wood veneer sealed with a plastic resin. Laminate flooring cannot be refinished. Some manufacturers offer click-together "floating" laminate floors and claim that theirs is an eco-friendly product because it doesn't require adhesive, but unless they also use low-VOC sealants and fiberboard with no added formaldehyde, it will still offgas.

Rubber

There are several types of rubber floor tiles, so ask about the raw materials before you buy. Pure rubber tiles or those with specs of cork incorporated are great in laundry rooms, kitchens, and bathrooms, and they come in vivid colors. If you find black rubber tiles with specks of bright colors, they are most likely made from recycled tire rubber. Given that this product uses recycled material, it is in some ways eco-friendly, but the tire rubber, binding, and specks of virgin EPDM (ethylene propylene diene monomer) rubber that add color can be sources of indoor air pollutants and VOCs. All rubber tiles are highly durable, resist water, and prevent slips, but the ones that offgas are best installed outdoors.

Tile

Offering more colors, patterns, shapes, and materials than one can imagine, tile offers limitless design opportunities. It's also a fairly low-impact choice, even though some kinds do require a moderate amount of energy to produce.

For a more eco-friendly floor, look for tile that incorporates recycled material. Handmade Debris Series terra-cotta tiles from Fireclay incorporate granite dust and recycled glass. Concrete tiles require less energy to make because they don't have to be fired, and there are lots of styles to choose from. You can find concrete tiles that contain recycled glass, pre-consumer stone waste, and fly ash. There are

even metal tiles made from recycled aluminum. Recycled-glass tiles are becoming easier to source—some manufacturers melt down recycled glass and add pigments, while others melt down colored glass without any additives. If you're looking at natural-stone tile, try to find a variety that was quarried close to your home rather than something shipped from halfway around the world.

Where there's tile, there's grout, and some people have a strong adverse reaction to it. While tile itself is generally long lasting and low maintenance, grout needs to be kept sealed to prevent staining. Choose a low-VOC, water-based sealant.

LEFT Concrete tiles laid diagonally are broken up by strips of dark-stained hardwood.

RIGHT Blue and white glazed ceramic tiles are kept small on a bathroom floor so there's enough grout to prevent slips.

Terrazzo

Traditionally poured on-site, terrazzo is basically a concrete floor with little pieces of stone mixed in. The surface is then troweled and polished to reveal its colorful embedded pieces. Tiles are available if you want the look without the price and hassle of the poured-in-place version. Ask your contractor to use pieces of recycled glass and porcelain if you're creating the floor from scratch, or look for terrazzo tiles that incorporate recycled materials. Most forms of terrazzo need to be kept sealed or waxed to prevent stains.

Concrete

Another choice generally reserved for new construction is concrete. Many homeowners find concrete to be an easy-to-maintain option that fits the style of modern structures. It's also extremely versatile in that it can be colored, stamped, stained, and textured. You can even add bits of stone aggregate for a more slip-resistant floor. Just because concrete can look unfinished, don't assume a concrete floor is inexpensive, especially if you add decorative details.

Floors like concrete, tile, and terrazzo can be cold underfoot, which is why people usually pair them with a hydronic radiant-heat system or, in small applications, electric heat mats. Architect Peter Pfeiffer has heard some complaints from people who have lived with concrete floors: "They say it's a hard and unforgiving surface, especially as people age and need more padding underfoot so that their joints don't start to ache."

CONTRACTOR
JASON LEAR ON

Dealing with Floor-Finishing Fumes

Whatever you finish your floor with, make sure you air out the space well. Even when we're using a soy-based concrete stain and sealant, we open up all the doors and windows and let the fumes out. And you can practically eat that stuff!"

LEFT This concrete floor was tinted with a nontoxic soy-based stain and is kept warm by a hydronic heat system installed underneath.

TOP RIGHT NuHeat radiant mats are a great way to heat up cold floors. During a remodel, they are inexpensive to install— and with solar panels generating your home's electricity, the mats could be heated at no cost.

MIDDLE RIGHT Terrazzo tiled floors can mimic the look of stone or add a punch of color to a room, as does the orange glass sprinkled within this tile.

BOTTOM RIGHT Concrete's practicality and durability make it a popular choice for flooring that is designed to flow from indoors to out.

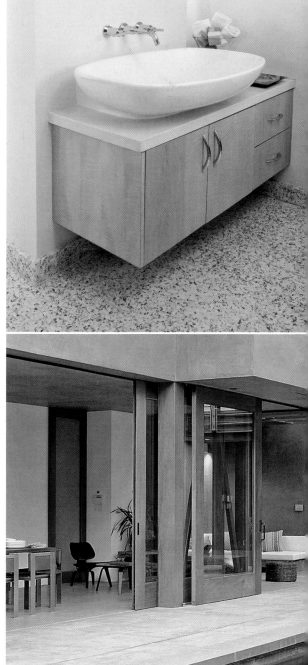

TOP Nature's Carpet makes untreated wall-to-wall wool carpeting with no chemical dyes and a natural rubber and jute backing.

BOTTOM Jute rugs have an interesting texture and naturally resist spills.

OPPOSITE PAGE Low-pile carpet tiles made of natural or recycled materials are a way to create a warm path around the bedroom without installing wall-to-wall carpet that traps dust and pollen.

Carpet

Despite the environmental and health concerns that have plagued this industry, carpet remains the most popular floor covering on the market. Most carpet fibers are nylon, polyolefin, or polyester, all of which are made from petrochemicals that are harmful to the environment during manufacturing and do not break down at the end of their life cycle. An estimated 5 billion pounds of carpet is thrown away each year, making this a major environmental issue.

Carpet backing and underlayment, usually made of PVC or styrene-butadiene (SB) latex, release harmful chemicals into your home that are what we think of as that "new-carpet smell." Beyond the dangerous materials and adhesives used in backing and underlayment, there are scores of chemicals applied to the carpet fiber for color, stain resistance, and preventing the growth of fungi and bacteria. Antimicrobials, in particular, have been scrutinized in recent years because they are a known hazardous material.

To address the nonbiodegradable issue, many companies have begun incorporating recycled content into their carpeting. The carpet manufacturer InterfaceFLOR has developed carpet tiles made of recycled material and will even take your old carpet tiles back to turn them into—you guessed it—more carpet.

Wool carpeting is the most eco-friendly plush carpet because it is biodegradable. But for good indoor air quality, be sure that the backing is made of natural rubber and jute; and if the wool came from another country, make sure it was not sprayed with chemical moth repellent when it entered this country (most wool is). Wool naturally resists stains, dust mites, mold, and mildew. Eco-friendly carpet manufacturers now offer safer underlayment materials as well—look for those made of untreated wool. Another option is to use carpet made of sustainable and renewable fibers, such as sisal, jute, hemp, or abaca. These rugs are beautiful but are not as soft as wool for sitting or playing.

Many large carpet manufacturers have taken steps to make their products healthier. When shopping in big-box stores and nationwide chains, look for specific lines of carpeting that meet Green Label Plus standards, which limit the amount of VOCs, formaldehyde, and other toxins. They do not, however, regulate flame retardants and perfluorocarbons.

Architect Eric Corey Freed discourages wall-to-wall carpet because it traps dust and allergens and is difficult to clean. If you buy eco-friendly carpeting for certain rooms, be sure to use green methods to clean it.

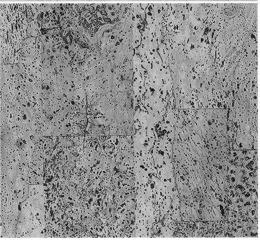

LEFT Wood offers a warm, natural look and is available in a wide range of species and colors.

Linoleum is the green alternative to vinyl. Mix colors for a unique pattern.

Some cork has pits in the surface that crumbs can fall into, but it's easy to clean with a vacuum.

Flooring at a glance

Wood

- **Pros:** Wide variety of species, colors, grains, and plank widths; warm underfoot; can be sanded and refinished several times.
- **Cons:** Some types are not rated for use over radiant-heat floors; must be kept dry.
- **Price:** $–$$$
- **Installation:** Installation best left to a professional; available as nail-down, glue-down, or floating flooring.
- **Green issues:** Buy FSC-certified or reclaimed wood flooring; use water-based, low- or no-VOC stains and finishes.

Bamboo

- **Pros:** Sustainable; less expensive than hardwood; solid bamboo can be sanded and refinished several times; woven bamboo is extremely hard and durable.
- **Cons:** Limited color choices; horizontal-grain bamboo does not hide dents well.

- **Price:** $–$$
- **Installation:** Installs just like hardwood.
- **Green issues:** Importation from Asia produces carbon emissions; avoid manufacturers that use formaldehyde-based resins and adhesives and high-VOC finishes.

Cork

- **Pros:** Warm and soft underfoot; resists denting; has insulating qualities.
- **Cons:** Must be kept dry.
- **Price:** $–$$
- **Installation:** DIY-friendly.
- **Green issues:** Uses a renewable and post-industrial waste material; avoid manufacturers that use formaldehyde-based adhesives and high-VOC finishes.

Linoleum

- **Pros:** Wide variety of colors; made of natural materials; durable; biodegradable; warm and soft underfoot.

- **Cons:** Linseed oil in linoleum gives off a slight odor that some people find objectionable (decreases over time).
- **Price:** $–$$
- **Installation:** DIY-friendly.
- **Green issues:** Currently manufactured only in Europe, so importation results in carbon emissions.

Laminate

- **Pros:** Looks similar to hardwood, ceramic, or stone but can be less expensive.
- **Cons:** Damaged pieces will need to be replaced as they cannot be refinished.
- **Price:** $–$$
- **Installation:** Challenging DIY installation; can float over existing subfloor.
- **Green issues:** Most brands are made with fiberboard cores that contain urea-formaldehyde and do not use low-VOC finishes.

LEFT Fast-growing bamboo and coconut palm reduce the need to cut down mature trees for wood flooring.

RIGHT With glass or stone, terrazzo tiles can incorporate practically any color.

Rubber

- **Pros:** Durable; resists water and prevents slips; wide variety of colors.
- **Cons:** Certain types made with recycled tires have an odor; some styles are more suited to commercial and outdoor installations.
- **Price:** $–$$
- **Installation:** DIY-friendly.
- **Green issues:** Look for manufacturers that use pure rubber with no toxic additives; if recycled material is used, make sure it won't offgas.

Tile

- **Pros:** Broad range of materials, including ceramic, glass, concrete, stone, and porcelain; durable; water-resistant.
- **Cons:** Must choose styles that are rated for floor use; can be slippery; cold underfoot; grout is high-maintenance.
- **Price:** $–$$$
- **Installation:** DIY-friendly.
- **Green issues:** Look for tiles made of recycled materials or for salvaged or surplus tiles; choose locally quarried stone or substitute with porcelain.

Terrazzo

- **Pros:** Durable and waterproof.
- **Cons:** Heavy; cold and hard underfoot; unless a resin binder was used, tiles need to be kept sealed.
- **Price:** $$–$$$
- **Installation:** Tiles install like any others; if poured in place, terrazzo requires an experienced professional.
- **Green issues:** Choose varieties that contain pre- or post-consumer recycled glass or other recycled materials rather than new stone.

Concrete

- **Pros:** Can be stamped, textured, and colored.
- **Cons:** Cold and hard underfoot (usually warmed up by a radiant-heat system); must be resealed regularly to avoid stains.
- **Price:** $$–$$$
- **Installation:** Hire an experienced contractor.
- **Green issues:** Ask your contractor to substitute some of the Portland cement with fly ash to reduce CO_2 emissions by keeping fly ash out of landfills.

Carpet

- **Pros:** Soft and warm underfoot.
- **Cons:** Difficult to keep clean; most types are not biodegradable and will offgas; limited colors in the most eco-friendly lines.
- **Price:** $–$$
- **Installation:** Wall-to-wall carpeting requires professional installation.
- **Green issues:** Choose carpet made of natural materials that haven't been stain-proofed or moth-proofed, and make sure the backing and underlayment materials don't offgas; carpet containing recycled material is another option.

Wall Treatments

A harmonious color palette and geometric shapes turn this wall of cabinets into the focal point of the room.

Think of your walls as the backdrop for the design of your room. Depending on the look you're going for, you may want something bold like stark white, a highly saturated color, or a funky pattern. Or you may want a soft neutral that plays a supporting role. There are eco-friendly options for all of the standard wall treatments, including paint, plaster, wainscot, wallpaper, and tile.

Paint

Adding a fresh coat of paint is one of the least expensive ways to improve the look of a room, so it's one of the most popular home improvement projects. When you buy paint, you are expected to know three things to place your order: the color you want, the sheen (flat, eggshell, semigloss, or high gloss), and whether you prefer oil or latex. But today, you can also choose low- or no-VOC paint.

Traditional Choices: Oil and Latex

Oil-based paint contains high amounts of VOCs that release into the air while you're painting and for months after. Plus the toxins will attach to breathable materials in the house, such as upholstery and drapes, where they will continue to offgas over time.

All paint contains pigment (color), solvent to make the paint easy to work with and help it dry, and binding agents that make the paint stick to vertical surfaces. The solvents used in oil-based paint can include benzene, formaldehyde, toluene, and xylene, which are carcinogens or neurotoxins. There are also mineral spirits incorporated to slow drying time, which some painters prefer. According to the Environmental Protection Agency, when you are using this kind of paint, you may experience lung irritation, dizziness, or vision problems, and long-term exposure (experienced by professional painters and construction workers) can also damage the nervous system, liver, and kidneys. Some chemicals found in oil-based paint have been shown to cause cancer or reproductive and developmental defects in laboratory animals. Pregnant women, young children, and the elderly and infirm should avoid breathing fumes from oil-based paint.

Water-based paint, also called latex, uses water as its main solvent. Water-based paint emits lower levels of VOCs, making it a healthier choice overall, but many brands still contain formaldehyde, acrylonitrile, ethylene glycol ethers, fungicides, and preservatives—all stuff you really don't want to breathe or release into the atmosphere. Water-based paint dries faster than oil-based paint, and it cleans up with soap and water.

TOP Warm red walls frame large windows that let the colors of nature take center stage.

RIGHT A favorite antique or piece of art can inspire your color choices.

BOTTOM Natural light shines down on a freestanding tub surrounded by crisp ceramic tiles and soothing lavender-painted walls.

No-VOC and Low-VOC Paint

Oil-based versus water-based used to be the only choice in paint, but now there are companies making interior and exterior no-VOC latex paints that are extremely low-odor and do not contain the harmful chemicals or solvents listed on the previous page. The one catch is that when the paint store adds pigment to a gallon of white no-VOC paint, that pigment is usually oil-based and will therefore add VOCs to the paint. So be sure to ask about the pigment used. If you want truly no-VOC paint, you'll often need to find a local green building-supply store that uses no-VOC pigments when mixing paint to order, or a manufacturer that offers premixed no-VOC colors.

Many national paint companies now offer low- and no-VOC paints in their stores. No-VOC paints are high performing, durable, and completely safe for pregnant women and babies to be around, so always try to go with the healthiest choice. In addition, several small, independent paint manufacturers make only no-VOC paint, including Yolo Colorhouse, AFM Safecoat, American Pride, and Mythic.

Plant-Based and Milk Paints

Beyond latex-based paint, there are plant-based and milk paints. Neither type uses petrochemicals, and both are safe for you and the environment. People who are particularly sensitive to chemicals found in latex-based paint often prefer no-VOC milk-based paint, which is composed of milk protein, lime, clay, and nontoxic lead-free pigments. It has a bit of a dappled look that resembles old plaster and no sheen once it's dry. Milk-based paint comes in powder form and is hand-mixed by you instead of the paint store. You can create a thin wash or a thick paint, and once mixed, it will stay fresh for up to a month if you keep it refrigerated.

Plant-based paints use non-petroleum-based binders and additives, and mineral pigments for color. They are nontoxic, but can produce temporary odors from nonchemical substances such as citrus oil or soy resin. If you have a chemically sensitive or asthmatic person in your home, always test a small amount of the paint before committing to an entire wall. Both plant-based and milk-based paints allow the surfaces they cover to breathe, which can be good for painting wood furniture but not as good when used in a room where mold and mildew can occur, such as bathrooms and kitchens.

TOP These are the colorants needed to tint a quart of paint of the purple color shown. Depending on the color you choose and where you buy the paint, there could be a large amount of high-VOC colorant added to your otherwise low- or no-VOC paint.

LEFT No-VOC paint will not pollute the air in your bedroom, keeping it the healthy sanctuary it should be while adding the color your design calls for.

OPPOSITE PAGE Milk paint gives walls instant patina.

ARCHITECT
ERIC COREY FREED ON

Choosing No-VOC Paint

We don't use low-VOC paints—only no-VOC. We don't even offer them to our clients as an option. I mean, if I were a chef and before I prepared a meal for you I asked if it was okay that I don't use cancer-causing ingredients, you'd think I was nuts. Like an organic chef prefers all the best, local, organic ingredients, we will always prefer the healthiest building materials. We spend so much time indoors that it's worth investing in them. We should have the equivalent of nutrition labels on every building product."

Recycled Paint

Need to paint a shed? Not particular about the color? There are companies that sell recycled paint for indoor and outdoor use. This is a great green choice because you'll be reusing something that would have been thrown away. You can also use recycled paint as a primer and cover it up with the color and finish you want. Recycled paints are usually water-based, but they can contain a wide variety of glosses and acrylics. If you're chemically sensitive, you might want to spend your green dollars elsewhere.

Plaster and Clay

Applying plaster or clay to your walls instead of paint gives them a tactile, breathable, natural finish. Look for products that use nontoxic mineral pigments to color natural clay, and post-industrial recycled aggregates. Because the color is integral, cracks

LEFT Mod Green Pod prints fabulous patterns on vinyl-free paper using low-impact inks. It also offers coordinating organic cotton fabric for custom draperies and bedding.

RIGHT There's an art to troweling on plaster. Hire an experienced professional or spend some time practicing on a scrap piece of drywall before attempting a larger area.

and nicks in the wall won't stand out. This is also a great solution for walls that have seen better days, as you're adding a thick layer that covers up the kind of damage that paint alone cannot. Plaster can be troweled onto many substrates, including primed drywall,

and it can be moistened and worked over and over again if you don't seal it. Because the product is porous, sealing is recommended in humid areas such as bathrooms and kitchens.

Wallpaper

Wallpaper is another way to add color and texture to a space. Most readily available wallpaper is made of paper-backed vinyl, fabric-backed vinyl, or expanded vinyl, because vinyl is more durable and easier to work with than plain paper types. However, vinyl is not an eco-friendly product (see pages 36–67). Vinyl wallpaper usually comes pre-pasted, and the glue offgases low levels of VOCs. Mold can easily grow underneath vinyl wallpaper without being noticed, and the mold spores cause a variety of additional environmental and health problems.

Fortunately, there are many eco-friendly wallpaper choices now on the

market that are vinyl-free. Look for those made of natural materials such as sisal, honeysuckle vines, and cork. Plus a growing number of designers are now printing with soy-based or low-impact inks on FSC-certified or recycled paper. Install wallpaper with a nontoxic adhesive such as 389 Natural Wallpaper Adhesive, made from all-natural plant-based materials, or a low-VOC water-based adhesive. On the Internet, you can find recipes for non-toxic, homemade wallpaper paste made mostly with ingredients you'll find in your kitchen cabinets.

If you need to remove old wallpaper, don't buy standard wallpaper remover. Use a steamer or a product called Wallwik, which contains no caustic chemicals. For your own safety, hire a professional to remove wallpaper if you find more than a few square inches of mold underneath.

Wainscot and Paneling

Wood wainscot (or wainscoting) is often seen in Arts and Crafts, cottage-style, and Victorian homes, though it is suitable in almost any design. In addition to wood, you can use ceramic, porcelain, or glass tiles for wainscot, which are easier to keep clean in bathrooms and mudrooms.

Buy FSC-certified wood wainscot and finish it with low-VOC stains and sealants. If you plan to paint the wainscot, you might be tempted by low-cost medium-density fiberboard (MDF), which stands up to moisture better than solid wood. But MDF contains formaldehyde that will offgas in your home, so look for MDF products with no added formaldehyde, such as Medex by Columbia Forest Products, and finish them with no-VOC primer and paint. Wheatboard, made from wheat stalks left over after the edible part of the plant is harvested, is another MDF substitute that has no added formaldehyde. Also be sure to use low-VOC, water-based adhesives to glue wainscot to the wall.

There are many new wall-panel products made of eco-friendly materials that can also be installed one-third or two-thirds of the way up a wall like wainscot. They include bamboo, Kirei board, and durapalm (made from reclaimed plantation-grown palms).

TOP LEFT Kirei makes these wall tiles and panels out of reclaimed coconut shells, low-VOC resins, and FSC-certified wood backing.

TOP MIDDLE Traditional painted beadboard complements Shaker-style furniture and face-frame cabinetry.

TOP RIGHT Floor-to-ceiling horizontal wood paneling painted in alternating stripes of white and green has a beachy, tropical feel.

BOTTOM LEFT Bamboo paneling from Plyboo gives walls visual texture and sustainable style.

BOTTOM RIGHT This wainscot was custom-milled from Medex, a wood-composite panel product with no added formaldehyde that resists moisture, making it ideal for bathrooms.

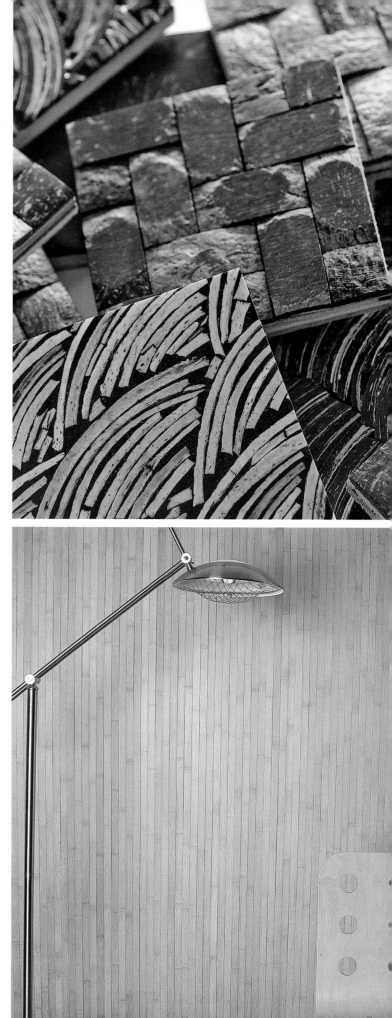

ARCHITECT MATT ELLIOTT ON

Northeast Style

In Maine, we have a bias for using real wood because it's such a staple here. We usually get locally grown maple and birch for interior trim such as wainscot and then finish it with no-VOC paint. There's a long history of painted cabinetry and trim work in the Northeast, so many people are drawn to that look over stained wood."

Tile

You can use all the same types of tiles for floors (see pages 36–40) on walls, plus more delicate versions and relief tiles. Look for ceramic tiles that include recycled content, and tiles made from post-consumer recycled glass. Sandhill Industries says each of its recycled-glass tiles takes one-half the energy to produce as ceramic tile. Bedrock Industries does not use any pigment in its recycled-glass tiles, and the results are bright and punchy.

If you want stone-tiled walls, choose a stone that is quarried locally. Most granite and marble come from South America, India, and Scandinavia and are processed into tiles and slabs in Italy. It can be tough to find locally quarried stone in many parts of the country. Maine currently has operating granite quarries, so local architect Matt Elliott uses this low-cost material in the houses he builds—for everything from fireplace surrounds to tiles to countertops. Also consider porcelain, which can mimic

LEFT Handmade ceramic tiles around a fireplace meet up with a horizontal-grain-bamboo mantel. Sweet potato orange low-VOC paint makes the whole thing pop.

RIGHT These cork mosaic tiles are a modern spin on ceramic penny-rounds.

the look of stone, or terrazzo tiles that incorporate recycled glass. Their patterns can look similar to granite.

Cork and Metal

In tile or sheet form, cork and metal are two more eco-friendly wall-covering options. There is no shortage of metal from old appliances, cars, and manufacturing waste to create tiles. Recycled-aluminum tiles can be found in several finishes and colors that can be used on

countertops in addition to walls. You can also find brushed metal and relief patterns in metal panels and tiles.

Take advantage of cork's acoustical properties by installing it on the walls of a playroom or bedroom. Cork's natural colors and patterns create a soft and textural wall surface. Most cork tiles come in 12-by-12-inch pieces, but it's possible to find rectangular shapes and even cork mosaic penny-rounds. Choose a brand that uses formaldehyde-free binders.

LEFT In a great juxtaposition of old and new, large punched-aluminum wall tiles set off this vintage console sink.

RIGHT Recycled-glass tiles can be tinted, or their color can come from the original glass. They are available in all standard tile sizes, including mosaics and borders.

CLOCKWISE FROM LEFT
This textural grasscloth wallpaper is made from plant fibers.

Plaster walls covered in no-VOC paint.

Cork tiles help absorb sound in a room.

Wall Treatments at a glance

Paint

- **Pros:** Quick and inexpensive.
- **Cons:** Won't cover up damage on a wall.
- **Price:** $
- **Installation:** Great DIY project.
- **Green issues:** Buy low-VOC (less than 50 grams per liter) or no-VOC paint for healthier indoor air quality.

Plaster and Clay

- **Pros:** Provides a breathable surface with integral color; covers up wall damage.
- **Cons:** Needs to be sealed in humid rooms.
- **Price:** $$
- **Installation:** Best left to a professional, though it can be learned with practice.
- **Green issues:** Buy brands that use mineral pigments and recycled materials.

Wallpaper

- **Pros:** Adds color and texture to walls; patterns available for all home styles.
- **Cons:** If moisture gets behind wallpaper, you can have a mold problem without knowing it.
- **Price:** $–$$$
- **Installation:** Mid-level DIY project.
- **Green issues:** Stay away from vinyl; look for wallpapers made from recycled paper and low-impact inks; use water-based or homemade adhesives.

Wainscot and Paneling

- **Pros:** Many materials can be used as wainscot; hides old damage and protects walls from new damage.
- **Cons:** Wood wainscot must be kept sealed to prevent moisture or termite damage.
- **Price:** $–$$$
- **Installation:** Mid-level DIY project; wood goes up quickly if you're using panels.
- **Green issues:** Buy natural materials, MDF (medium-density fiberboard) panels that do not contain formaldehyde, or reclaimed or FSC-certified wood; finish with a low- or no-VOC paint or stain.

Ceramic Tile

- **Pros:** Broad range of sizes, shapes, and colors; durable; water-resistant.
- **Cons:** Grout is high maintenance.
- **Price:** $–$$
- **Installation:** Mid-level DIY project; look for low-VOC tile adhesive and thin-set mortar.
- **Green issues:** Buy tiles that are made of or include recycled materials, or salvaged or surplus tiles that would otherwise go to waste.

LEFT Pair recycled-glass wall tiles with a countertop that also incorporates recycled glass.

TOP RIGHT Fireclay's Debris Series tiles are made from recycled glass and gravel, as well as asphalt waste material.

BOTTOM RIGHT Aside from having some of the best earth-toned colors on the market, Yolo Colorhouse offers poster-size samples painted in an eggshell finish so you can see what the color looks like at home without buying a quart.

Glass Tile

- **Pros:** Stylish; you can use larger glass tiles on walls than on floors because slip resistance isn't a factor.
- **Cons:** Grout is high maintenance.
- **Price:** $$–$$$
- **Installation:** Mid-level DIY project; use smooth, white thinset mortar, because you may be able to see through the tile.
- **Green issues:** Look for tiles made of recycled glass.

Stone Tile

- **Pros:** Luxurious; range of colors and patterns.
- **Cons:** Heavy; must be resealed regularly.
- **Price:** $$–$$$
- **Installation:** Mid-level DIY project, unless the pieces are large, in which case best left to a professional.
- **Green issues:** Most varieties are shipped in from overseas, contributing to carbon emissions; choose one quarried close to home or substitute porcelain or terrazzo.

Cork Tile

- **Pros:** Natural acoustical qualities; adds color and texture to walls; tiles without grout.
- **Price:** $–$$$
- **Installation:** Mid-level DIY project; use water-based, low- or no-VOC contact adhesive on smooth, flat walls.
- **Green issues:** Buy cork tiles prefinished with no-VOC sealant and with no added formaldehyde binders.

Metal Tile

- **Pros:** High-end and modern.
- **Cons:** Some finishes show fingerprints easily.
- **Price:** $$–$$$
- **Installation:** Mid-level DIY project; use a metal cutting blade on a tile saw.
- **Green issues:** Look for manufacturers that use scrap metal that would otherwise end up in a landfill.

Furniture

Eco-friendly furniture doesn't have to be expensive. Find old wicker barstools like these and give them new life with two coats of no-VOC paint. Healthful upholstered furniture is available in styles that are at home in everything from beach cottages to formal living rooms.

Just like floor and wall coverings, the furniture that we sit on and live with can be made with materials that are bad for the environment and our health. Couches are often filled with petrochemical-based foam and covered in toxic flame and stain retardants. Wooden tables and chairs are coated in oil-based finishes, and low-cost furniture made of particleboard or MDF offgasses formaldehyde. There's a certain smell we associate with newness when we get a piece of furniture delivered, but that smell is negatively affecting our indoor air quality. Fortunately, a number of conscientious furniture companies are coming to the rescue by making furniture of FSC-certified wood, nontoxic finishes, and organic upholstery.

Upholstery

While a good deal of attention has been given to unhealthful materials in mattresses, not much has been reported about upholstered furniture. It's really the same issue. Makers of traditional upholstered furniture use an inexpensive flame retardant called polybrominated diphenyl ether (PBDE), which has been linked to developmental and neurological defects, impaired reproductive systems, altered concentrations of thyroid hormones, and hyperactivity in studies of lab animals. PBDE has been found in human breast milk, and unborn children and infants are most at risk. While the most toxic forms of PBDEs, called octa and penta, have been discontinued, deca PBDE is still being used. A limited ban on deca PBDEs has been instituted in some states, but chemical companies have stalled compliance while trying to find another inexpensive way to flameproof furniture and mattresses.

A natural, chemical-free flame retardant does exist, and it's called wool. But wool is expensive and not manmade, so it isn't considered a universal solution to the problem. You can, however, buy upholstered furniture today that meets flame-retardancy laws by using specially woven wool that slows down flames just as well as PBDE does. Harmful chemicals will continue to be used in upholstered furniture until consumers demand that they not be.

Cushions

Most sofa cushions contain polyurethane foam, which is made with toluene diisocyanate, a possible carcinogen that contributes to air pollution. Some companies augment polyurethane foam with soy foam, but currently they can't go beyond 20 percent because of the strong odor of this material. The healthiest, greenest choice for cushions is rubber with no chemical additives, but it costs much more than foam.

Better Choices

So what should you look for in eco-friendly upholstered furniture? Choose a company that uses FSC-certified frames; low- or no-VOC wood finishes on the exposed wood; formaldehyde-free adhesives or no adhesives; pure rubber with no chemical additives; organic cotton and wool tufting; and green fabrics such as organic cotton, wool, hemp, and bamboo. Sometimes you can find local furniture makers or custom upholstery shops that will create an eco-friendly product for you, but there are also furniture companies dedicated to this cause that make beautiful, functional furniture, such as Cisco Brothers, Q Collection, and EKLA Home.

Some people are concerned about not stain-proofing upholstered furniture. Don't let this worry stop you from buying healthy furniture for your family. Keep chemical-free furniture clean by incorporating a washable slipcover, or schedule regular visits with a nontoxic upholstery-cleaning service.

ABOVE There are a growing number of organic textiles in lovely colors and graphic prints that are suitable for upholstered furniture.

LEFT This velvety club chair from Q Collection was designed with style and indoor air quality in mind.

RIGHT Los Angeles–based Cisco Brothers creates sustainable upholstered furniture using FSC-certified hardwoods, water-based glues, and eco-friendly fabrics.

Wood

Like wood flooring, wooden furniture uses a precious natural resource that cleans the air and must be preserved if our environment has any chance of rehabilitation. By choosing FSC-certified wood furniture, you can support the efforts of companies that are not cutting down old-growth trees or clear-cutting forests. Or buy furniture made with locally grown wood that's harvested in a sustainable way. Also be sure that the manufacturer uses low- or no-VOC stains and sealants.

There is an abundance of wood from torn-down buildings that can be used to make gorgeous wooden furniture, and many artists and designers are doing just that. Furniture made from reclaimed wood can be any style, from clean-lined modern to distressed and rustic. Furniture made from locally reclaimed wood is best, though you can also find options that were made overseas.

Secondhand Furniture

Reusing products that are no longer wanted is the best green option, as you're keeping something out of the landfill that may not be made of biodegradable materials. And the offgassing will be greatly reduced by the time you get the piece of furniture. So unless you are extremely sensitive to chemicals, or are allergic to the stain or flame retardants on the upholstery, you should be able to live with the furniture without negative health effects.

Mix in furniture that you find at estate sales or antique stores with new eco-friendly pieces. While some may include materials you would rather not have in your house, you are doing the world a service by putting a piece that already exists to good use. When a chair or couch has seen better days, have it reupholstered with eco-friendly, untreated fabrics. You may also choose to replace foam cushions with natural rubber.

Old furniture might be covered with lead-based paint. As long as you don't disturb the paint by sanding it, the lead will stay in place and not pose any harm. But if you have pets or children, it's best to coat the pieces with a low-VOC polyurethane finish to seal the old paint in place. You can pick up a lead-paint test kit from a home improvement center to see whether you need to take precautionary measures.

TOP LEFT Scouring estate sales is well worth the effort if you can come up with a vignette like this.

BOTTOM LEFT Ultra-rustic reclaimed-wood stools complement the reclaimed ceiling beams and vent-hood trim.

TOP MIDDLE Look for individual used pieces that have a similar shape or size to make a cohesive new set.

BOTTOM RIGHT Think creatively about how to use discarded pieces. These old library carts are put to good use as magazine holders.

TOP RIGHT This 8-foot-long table was made from scaffolding used when the house was being remodeled. It continues contributing to the home and serves as a reminder of those dusty renovation days.

Decorative Accessories

Artists and designers are finding great inspiration creating home accessories out of eco-friendly materials. There are bowls, placemats, towels, and sheets made of bamboo; plates, bowls, and night-lights made of recycled glass; placemats, wastebaskets, and bags made of old candy wrappers and billboard posters; candlesticks and bowls made of recycled aluminum; and much more in any category you can think of.

THROW PILLOWS add color and pattern to a room and can dress up neutral couches and bedding. Designers are now using fabulous organic cotton prints to make healthier throw pillows, but make sure the ones you buy are also filled with eco-friendly

materials as opposed to standard synthetic down or poly-fill. Pillows filled with organic cotton are light and fluffy, while wool-filled pillows have a more solid feel. You can also find throw pillows stuffed with kapok, a tree fiber, or with woven corn fiber. Both have great loft. Consider making throw-pillow cases out of 100 percent natural fiber remnant fabric, but first wash the material three times with baking soda and vinegar to remove any sprayed-on flame and stain retardant b chemicals (test on a small spot first).

PLANTS bring a bit of nature indoors, and some can even clean the air you breathe. If you have something in your house

LEFT The owner of this house sees beauty in things that often get thrown away. For wall art, he used everything from recycled-metal sculpture to food wrappers to an old cowboy hat.

ABOVE RIGHT Throw pillows made with organic cotton and nontoxic inks, stuffed with kapok or other natural fibers, are the perfect complement to an organic sofa.

RIGHT Set an air-cleaning plant like this peace lily in a room and within days you will notice the difference.

FAR RIGHT An old chemistry set holds blooming rosebuds.

that you fear is offgassing, add plants to counteract it. You'll want two or three plants per 60 square feet; not all of them need to be near a window. Consult a local plant guide for more information.

Among the most effective air purifiers are the following:

Areca palm	Janet Craig dracaena
Australian sword fern	Peace lily
Boston fern	Reed palm
Dwarf date palm	Rubber plant
English ivy	Weeping fig

WALL ART can be found in an array of recycled materials, from used oil drums to wood that has washed up from the ocean. Look for pieces that are not coated with oil-based finishes. If they are made in third-world countries, as many are, make sure they bear a fair-trade label. Almost anything can be turned into wall art. Search your local salvage yard for interesting architectural pieces.

CANDLES add mood lighting to any room, but they can be bad for indoor air quality. Standard candles are made of paraffin, which is petroleum-based. Instead, choose beeswax or soy candles with all-natural cotton wicks. Added scents should be derived from essential oils and botanical ingredients.

BOWLS AND SERVING PLATTERS can be made of recycled glass, reclaimed wood, natural slate, bamboo, and cork. You don't need to be as stringent with decorative bowls that won't come into contact with food, but be sure plates and other dishes that will hold food are finished with safe sealants.

PHOTOGRAPHS make any room more personal. Instead of buying all new frames, collect used ones in every shape and color, then paint them so the different colors won't detract attention from the images. Or stick to a consistent theme, like all gold or a mixture of gold and silver. You can also find frames made of recycled wood and other reused materials.

INTERIOR DESIGNER
KELLY LAPLANTE ON

Using Vintage Accessories

I love using vintage dishes to create a juxtaposition with a modern-style table. I'll pair recycled-metal place settings with a set of antique dishes, and the combination looks awesome. Be aware that some vintage china does have lead in it, so to be safe, you should eat off glass plates."

LEFT New plates made of recycled glass are paired with midcentury silverware, a branch from the garden, and soy candles.

TOP RIGHT Vintage gold frames found over the years create a one-of-a-kind memory wall.

MIDDLE RIGHT Show off a collection of Depression-era glass and porcelain serving pieces on open shelves.

BOTTOM RIGHT Not quite ready to convert your old wood-burning fireplace to gas? Burning soy candles in the fireplace brings the romance without the soot.

Chapter 3

Kitchens and Baths

Each year, hundreds of thousands of people decide to update their kitchens and bathrooms, resulting in the purchase of massive amounts of building and finishing materials. This chapter will outline your buying choices so you can make the components of your remodel more eco-friendly. Beyond choosing from the types of cabinets, countertops, and fixtures discussed in these pages, be sure to hire contractors who share in your green vision. Take this opportunity to add more insulation than the building code requires, and try to use as many recycled and low-VOC materials as possible.

This tiny kitchen is packed with eco-friendly materials. Reclaimed madrone butcher-block countertops and veneered cabinets by Core Casework are finished with natural hardwax oil. The original fir floor was refinished and painted with low-VOC paint and polyurethane sealant.

TOP The owners of this coastal Maine farmhouse banned PVC plastic from their remodel and created a sustainable, energy-efficient home using local materials with the help of architect Matt Elliott. Local granite countertops sit atop no-added-formaldehyde cabinets finished with low-VOC paint.

BOTTOM LEFT Vetrazzo takes glass from curbside recycling programs and mixes it with concrete to create striking and unique countertops.

BOTTOM RIGHT A dual-flush toilet, recycled glass tiles, concrete sink, certified wood cabinetry and doors, and no-VOC paint make this powder room efficient and sustainable.

Cabinets

A bamboo-topped island is a relatively inexpensive addition to a kitchen that needs more countertop and storage space.

K itchen and bathroom cabinets can be a big investment in time, money, and materials. Traditionally, cabinet boxes are made of plywood or particleboard, while door and drawer faces are made of plywood or solid wood. The cabinets are then finished with oil-based enamels and stains, either in a factory (for stock or semicustom cabinets) or in your home (for custom cabinets). Although it can be a bit more expensive, it's worth seeking out sustainable and healthful alternatives to the standard way of building and finishing cabinetry, given how much raw material is being used and the impact it will have on your indoor air quality.

Using What You Have

Before surveying all the material options for new cabinets, strongly consider keeping the ones you have. This is the most eco-friendly way to remodel your kitchen or bath. It's a realistic option if the layout still works for you, but you just don't like the color of the cabinets. Clean and repaint cabinets with no-VOC paint and protect the new paint with a low-VOC clear sealer. Or sand, stain, and seal solid-wood cabinets. If you don't like the style of the doors and drawer faces, you can order FSC-certified replacements and refinish the existing boxes.

ARCHITECT
MICHELLE KAUFMANN ON

Kitchen Islands

I love big islands in a kitchen. They're usually the heart of the room, where you can prep meals and commune with family and guests. So most of the kitchens in the homes I build are designed around the island, while the cabinets and appliances support it. We also use a lot of drawers in kitchens, rather than shelves, as they seem the most efficient way to stay organized."

All the bells and whistles of new cabinetry can be incorporated into existing cabinetry, such as recycling bins, spice racks, and lazy susans. Replace old hinges and drawer slides if needed, add new hardware, and you'll have new-looking cabinets at a fraction of the cost to you and the environment.

If there's a section of cabinets that you'd like to replace with a new appliance, or a wall that needs to be removed, you can take out that section carefully and donate the cabinets to a salvage yard. You may also be able to reuse the cabinets in another part of the room or in the garage. Need more storage space? Consider adding an island, open shelves, or a piece of freestanding furniture.

TOP LEFT You can incorporate recycling bins and integrated food-storage containers into existing cabinetry to make it more functional.

TOP RIGHT Instead of replacing the bathroom vanity, add storage by building a recessed cabinet between studs in the wall for small toiletries and makeup.

BOTTOM When built-in cabinets are out of your budget, look for used freestanding cabinets and tables to equip your kitchen. The owner of this home used old metal cages for dishes and glassware.

Green inside and out, these cabinets are made of wheatboard with no added formaldehyde and are finished with low-VOC paint. Other eco-friendly features in this kitchen include cork flooring and a salvaged range.

Style and Function

If you're in the market for brand-new cabinetry, you may worry that eco-friendly options just won't look right in your house. But remember our mantra: Green is not a style. Yes, you can use bamboo veneer, Kirei board, or other natural-looking green materials, but you can also use FSC-certified wood and plywood without added formaldehyde to build cabinets in any style and design you want. Even the most traditional-looking cabinets can be 100 percent green.

In addition to deciding on a design, spend a good amount of time figuring out how you want your kitchen or bathroom to function. Make these rooms as accessible as possible using universal-design principles (see page 10). While it's tempting to fill the space with as much storage as you can, take this opportunity to pare down and donate anything you haven't used in the past year to a local charity. Opt for a multipurpose island if you have the floor space instead of cramming the room with too many upper cabinets that will make it feel smaller and darker. Also consider supplementing built-in cabinets with freestanding-furniture—ideally, vintage or otherwise reclaimed pieces.

Materials

Built-in cabinetry is no place to skimp. You're about to invest in something that should be a part of the house for a long time. Buying inexpensive cabinets made of particleboard or MDF is not a long-term solution. These materials don't fare well when exposed to water or moisture (meaning they will need to be replaced sooner), not to mention their negative effect on indoor air quality.

In some areas, eco-friendly practices and materials may be difficult to find, but an increasing number of cabinetmakers are switching over to them. Seek out builders who truly believe that using FSC-certified wood and nontoxic finishes is the right way to do business, and who have invested time and energy in finding and learning how to work with the best materials.

CABINET BOXES, for cost and weight reasons, are not usually made of solid wood. You want to stay away from particle-board and MDF for the reasons given above, but plywood is a long-lasting option. Although standard plywood contains adhesives that include formaldehyde, you can find cabinet-makers who use a plywood product with soy-based adhesive that does not include formaldehyde and therefore won't offgas in your home. This type of plywood is commonly referred to as having no added formaldehyde, because while the adhesive doesn't have formaldehyde, there can be a very small amount of naturally occurring formaldehyde in raw wood. Therefore, it wouldn't be accurate to refer to most wood products as formaldehyde-free.

Wheatboard is another option for eco-friendly cabinet boxes. It comes in sheets and can be used just like other pressed-wood products, though it is actually pressed fiber made of wheat straw. Typically farmers would burn this inedible part of the wheat plant, which creates air pollution. Now this agri-waste material is being used to make cabinets and other furniture, and the manufacturers do not use formaldehyde binders. Interior designer Kelly LaPlante prefers using wheatboard cores for the cabinets she designs. "Just make sure that all of the edges are well sealed, because if water seeps into wheatboard, the material will expand," she explains.

TOP LEFT Simple, flat-panel doors in a floating cabinet are combined with open shelving. The countertop is made of reclaimed teak.

TOP RIGHT Vintage dressers can be turned into functional bathroom vanities. Coat existing paint with low-VOC polyurethane sealant to make the piece water-resistant and to cover up any old lead-based paint.

BOTTOM You would never know just by looking that the cabinets in this contemporary kitchen are made from plywood boxes with no added formaldehyde, along with FSC-certified cherry and low-VOC finishes.

DOORS AND DRAWERS can be made with FSC-certified wood, plywood with no added formaldehyde, wheatboard with an FSC-certified wood veneer, reclaimed wood, or bamboo. Avoid doors and drawers that use a plastic laminate or vinyl coating. You will be able to find a wide variety of FSC-certified wood species to provide the look you want.

Interested in door panels with glass inserts? It can be difficult to find recycled-glass panels for this use, but manufacturing glass is not an inherently high-energy process, so you should feel fine about using nonrecycled glass. There are companies that sell eco-friendly resin panels such as 3form, some of which have bamboo stalks or other decorative additions. Bamboo and Kirei board are also popular for door inserts. If you choose a tropical-wood panel insert, be sure it's FSC-certified.

Finishing Options
To protect your indoor air quality, finish the cabinets with low- or no-VOC paint and sealant, or stain and sealant,

LEFT This colorful kitchen is a great example of green design. Its elements create a harmonious and toxin-free space: cabinets of plywood with no added form-aldehyde and bamboo veneer finished with low-VOC sealant, composite counter-tops, recycled-glass backsplash tiles, concrete floors, and natural clay walls.

RIGHT Hardwax oil provides a natural, breathable finish that lets the true beauty of the wood shine through.

particularly if they are finished on-site. The enamels normally used to finish cabinets don't need a clear-coat sealant on top, but it's best to add one when using no- or low-VOC paint, as latex paint is not as scrubbable as enamel. If you buy stock or semicustom cabinets that are finished off-site using oil-based paints or stains, let them sit in the

garage for a month or so to offgas before bringing them into your home.

Some cabinetmakers will tell you that applying low- or no-VOC paint, stain, and sealant is more difficult than applying the products they are used to working with: Drying time is different, new spray tips are often needed, and it takes a skilled craftsman to create the clear, smooth finish that comes easily with enamels and oil-based finishes. But don't let these complaints stop you from getting the finish you want. There are cabinetmakers who have invested the time and resources to be able to provide beautiful and durable finishes using healthier materials. Some are listed in our Resources guide (see pages 202–203).

Several members of our design panel, including architect Paula Baker-Laporte and contractor Jason Lear, are proponents of natural oil finishes. They recommend them for clients who love the look of wood and don't want a glossy, plastic

finish like polyurethane covering it up. Natural oil penetrates the surface and protects wood from water and stains, allowing the wood to breathe and giving it a matte finish. Made of plant oils and waxes, some brands, such as Osmo, use mineral spirits as a solvent, while others, such as Rubio Monocoat, do not.

"The VOCs as a percentage in Osmo are high compared with those of a low-VOC paint, but you use so little of the liquid to cover a surface that the total amount of VOCs released into the air is not as much as you might think," Lear says. "I still prefer it because it's a natural material and homeowners can retouch damaged areas themselves by just rubbing on a little more oil. In contrast, when you damage a cabinet or floor finished with polyurethane, you have to sand off an entire layer of sealant and refinish the whole area. With natural oil, you don't need to depend on experts for repairs," he explains.

Hardware

The knobs and pulls you choose for your cabinets can reinforce the design you're going for or make a statement of their own. To make hardware as eco-friendly as possible, you'll first want to choose high-quality, long-lasting pieces. Generally these are the knobs and pulls that feel heavy and solid when you hold them. It's also best to buy hardware that isn't imported from far away to avoid the carbon emissions that produces. If possible, buy from local blacksmiths or artisans, or from those who use recycled metal, glass, cork, or eco-resins. Also choose knobs and pulls that are easy to grasp for people with limited hand strength.

TOP LEFT Cork inlay blends with the colors of the wood cabinetry and the metal pulls.

BOTTOM LEFT In a little girl's bathroom, these painted ceramic pulls add a touch of whimsy.

TOP RIGHT To create this look, go to a salvage yard and search through old crystal and milk-glass pulls.

BOTTOM RIGHT Sleek chrome bars can be grabbed and pulled with two hands, and they can hold hanging dish towels.

OPPOSITE PAGE Recycled-glass knobs and pulls by Spectra are set off by dark-stained cabinetry. The river rock backsplash continues the look of the concrete aggregate floor.

Countertops

If you're ready for something different and eco-friendly, you're in luck. There are a growing number of green options for countertops that are unique, innovative, and downright gorgeous.

Stone and Glass Composites

The most popular green countertops are composites, in which manufacturers use pre- and post-consumer recycled glass, porcelain, or stone in a concrete or polymer resin binder. Depending on the size of the composite material, the result can look similar to granite, or it can make a bolder statement.

Composite countertops that mix ground-up quartz or glass with polymers and pigments are nonporous and extremely durable. They contain a petrochemical-based binder that makes them virtually maintenance-free and requires no resealing to prevent stains. There are opposing viewpoints on these countertops regarding their merits as a green material. While the petrochemical-based binder is harmful to the environment during manufacturing and its eventual disposal, some feel this issue is balanced out by the fact that no additional chemical sealants are required over the life of the countertop. One manufacturer, CaesarStone, was recently certified by Greenguard, ensuring that any offgassing of the product while in your home is minimal. Quartz is generally a post-industrial, pre-consumer recycled material. If you choose a composite countertop that includes glass, look for one in which a high percentage of the glass is post-consumer recycled.

Vetrazzo, a company based in the San Francisco Bay Area, uses almost exclusively post-consumer glass, such as food and beverage bottles from curbside recycling programs. Vetrazzo's binder is a concrete mix that incorporates fly ash and uses no petrochemicals. Other products, such as IceStone and EnviroGLAS, also use recycled glass and concrete to make colorful and unique countertops. Because concrete is naturally porous, these countertop options made only of glass and concrete do need to be resealed occasionally to prevent staining. But a growing number of low-VOC sealants are available, and you can avoid having to reseal the countertops if you apply a thin coat of natural beeswax every four to five months. The wax protects the surface from stains and gives it a handsome patina over time.

ARCHITECT
PAULA BAKER-LAPORTE ON

Healthful Countertop Options

"Any solid-surface countertop is healthier than a countertop with grout lines, because the latter is difficult to keep clean. My favorite countertop material is slate because it's a natural product that can be found locally. While slate can chip, it cannot be stained. When I have a client for whom a bulletproof counter is required, I recommend CaesarStone. But if bulletproof is your first criterion, there will always be an environmental compromise."

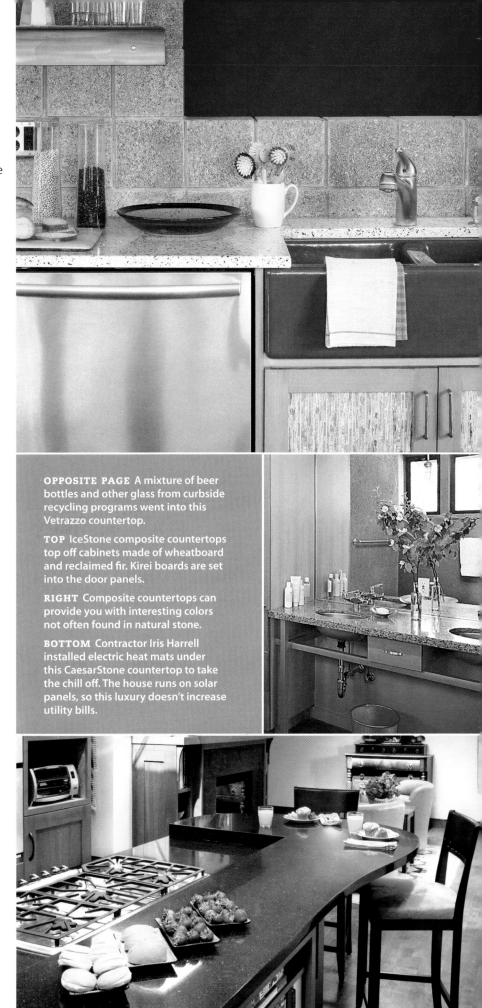

OPPOSITE PAGE A mixture of beer bottles and other glass from curbside recycling programs went into this Vetrazzo countertop.

TOP IceStone composite countertops top off cabinets made of wheatboard and reclaimed fir. Kirei boards are set into the door panels.

RIGHT Composite countertops can provide you with interesting colors not often found in natural stone.

BOTTOM Contractor Iris Harrell installed electric heat mats under this CaesarStone countertop to take the chill off. The house runs on solar panels, so this luxury doesn't increase utility bills.

Wood

Wood's natural beauty and warmth make it an appealing option as a countertop material. Wood countertops are an eco-friendly choice because they can be made locally out of FSC-certified or reclaimed materials, refinished if ever damaged, and reused or recycled when no longer needed as a countertop. Wooden-plank countertops, also referred to as face-grain, are not meant to be used as a cutting surface but they can work in both kitchens and bathrooms. Protect the surface from standing water, stains, and moisture with either a low-VOC polyurethane sealant or natural hardwax oil. If you want to cut on the surface, choose a butcher-block, or end-grain, counter that's made to withstand that kind of use, and treat it regularly with a food-safe oil. Wood countertops do require some maintenance, but there is freedom in knowing that stains or other light damage can be sanded out.

Bamboo

As discussed in the previous chapter, bamboo grows much faster than wood and requires less water and no fertilizer. But the Moso bamboo used for flooring and countertops is currently grown only in Asia, and a large amount of energy is required to manufacture and transport this material. Most bamboo countertops are bamboo veneer attached to a plywood base, although you can find solid-bamboo options. Look for those made with formaldehyde-free and food-safe adhesives. As with wood, you can finish bamboo countertops with either polyurethane or natural oil.

Stainless Steel

Restaurants and hospitals rely on stainless steel countertops because of their natural resistance to heat, water, rust, and bacteria. Stainless steel is an eco-friendly option because it can be recycled at the end of its life as a countertop, and new

OPPOSITE PAGE, LEFT Plaster walls combined with wooden cabinets and countertops finished with natural hardwax oil create an earthy, functional kitchen.

OPPOSITE PAGE, RIGHT Stainless steel around the sink and cooktop requires less maintenance, while wood warms up the island.

LEFT End-grain bamboo butcher block is a hard-working surface for a kitchen island.

RIGHT This curved wood counter acts as a base for the sink and a ledge for accessories.

sheets can be made of the recycled material. If you're not comfortable with water spots and scratches, you won't like polished stainless steel. Instead choose a brushed or matte finish. Look for heavy-duty steel (14- or 16-gauge) applied over plywood (with no added formaldehyde) to make it as quiet as possible.

ARCHITECT
PETER PFEIFFER ON

Why Countertop Colors Matter

I advise clients to pay attention to interior color selection because of the impact it has on lighting. More light will be required when it bounces off a dark surface. If you choose a light-colored or light-reflecting countertop, you'll need less electric lighting in your kitchen and will consume less energy overall."

Solid Surface

Made of plastic and mineral filler, solid-surface counters have enjoyed popularity for their range of available colors, low-maintenance attributes, and ability to create a seamless sink and counter surface. But these countertops are not recyclable or biodegradable, and the manufacturing process emits fumes from petrochemical-based materials, even though there is no offgassing once the material is installed in your home. Better to choose from among the growing number of plastic-free solid-surface options, such as PaperStone and EcoTop, that use recycled paper or bamboo fiber pressed and baked with nontoxic, water-based binders to produce an incredibly durable, stain-resistant surface. Like plastic-based countertops, pressed-paper countertops are not as heat-resistant as stone or composites. A pan heated to more than 350° will burn the material, but water can't harm it. As with wood countertops, any damage that occurs can be sanded away, as the color goes all the way through. Manufacturers offer varying levels of recycled material, so choose one with the most post-consumer recycled content available.

Concrete

Available precast or poured in place, concrete countertops can be tinted in earth-toned shades or bright colors. They generally have a mottled, matte finish, though gloss finishes are also possible. Make sure your cabinets and floors are strong enough to support them. You might have to reinforce the structure to hold the weight.

Poured-in-place concrete countertops are a messy proposition. You must ensure that dust and fumes inherent during the construction process are not spread throughout the house. It's better for your indoor air quality to bring in a precast concrete counter, but in situations where it's not logistically possible, the counter may have to be poured on-site. Architect Paula Baker-Laporte points out that while concrete countertops use a high amount of embodied energy, "so does a stone that's mined overseas. At least a poured-in-place concrete countertop didn't have to travel as far to get here."

Concrete is inherently porous and prone to hairline cracks. You can apply penetrating and topical sealants to prevent stains, and also beeswax to give an added layer of protection, but only people who are comfortable with a countertop surface that will eventually show its age should choose concrete.

FIBER CEMENT is a subcategory of concrete that has a similar aesthetic. Mixing cellulose fiber, fly ash, and other recycled materials with concrete can make it lighter and easier to transport. Manufactured off-site as precast slabs, fiber cement can include aggregate materials such as recycled glass and plastic or wood chips, or it can be a solid color. Because the main ingredient is still concrete, fiber-cement countertops are porous and need to be resealed or waxed regularly.

TOP LEFT Solid-surface countertops like PaperStone and Richlite have a matte finish that's warm to the touch. The material is equally at home in ultramodern kitchens and baths and more traditional designs.

TOP RIGHT Fiber-cement countertops weigh less than concrete but have the same natural, handmade look.

BOTTOM LEFT With the help of a how-to book and video, the owners of this remote cabin taught themselves how to make a concrete countertop. They even added a sloped area where wet dishes can drain into the sink.

BOTTOM RIGHT Pale wheat concrete countertops keep this room bright despite the gray concrete floors and cherry-stained cabinetry. Concrete tiles line the backsplash.

Natural Stone

Most natural stone sold today—including granite, marble, and limestone—is shipped in from Asia or Europe. Shipping something this heavy over such long distances results in a significant carbon footprint. Because of the extremely high demand for natural stone, particularly granite, we have been stripping the world of a natural resource. In a rush to supply natural stone to growing markets, many quarries have not taken proper ecological care, and workers are often not paid fairly. Recently, there have also been reports of high amounts of radon found in some granite counters.

If you must have a stone countertop, try to use a remnant from a fabricator or a recycled countertop from a building salvage yard so that you're making use of materials that have already made the trip here. In certain parts of the country, you may find a natural stone that's quarried locally, such as soapstone, slate, or granite along the East Coast.

Maintenance for stone countertops varies. Some types of granite don't need to be sealed, while softer marble and limestone are quite porous and need to be resealed regularly to prevent stains from cosmetics in the bathroom or from acids like lemon juice and tomato sauce in the kitchen.

Glass

Glass tiles make a pretty bathroom countertop and are available in glossy or honed finishes. Because glass is nonporous, like glazed ceramic, spills from food and chemicals won't harm the tiles, but you will have to maintain the grout.

You can also find solid sheets of recycled glass to use as countertop material, which is preferable to glass tiles in a kitchen. But glass is easily scratched and can be cracked, so you need to treat it carefully.

TOP Locally quarried New England soapstone was the perfect choice for this traditional Boston kitchen.

MIDDLE If you find a slab of marble at a used-building-supply store or salvage yard, a fabricator can use it to create a vintage-looking piece like this one.

BOTTOM Glass mosaic tiles spread across the countertop and climb up the wall, creating a shimmering sea of blue and white.

OPPOSITE PAGE A simple panel of recycled glass sitting on metal legs reflects the natural light streaming through translucent wall tiles.

ARCHITECT MATT ELLIOTT ON

Local Granite

Because the stone is quarried locally, I can get granite countertops in Maine for less money than a solid surface like Corian. The local granite generally comes in grays and pinks in a range of patterns. When you have an option that's durable, inexpensive, and local, people tend to favor it."

TOP Plain ceramic tiles are inexpensive, have a relatively low impact environmentally, and can be a long-lasting solution if a low-VOC sealant is applied to the grout regularly. In this bathroom, bull-nose pieces create a seamless edge.

BOTTOM With the front edge exposed, you can see the layers of plywood that comprise this plastic laminate counter. The self-rimming sink has a good bead of caulk around the edge to protect the plywood from water damage.

RIGHT Porcelain tile looks similar to stone but is much more durable for a kitchen countertop. It's paired here with iridescent glass mosaic tiles on the backsplash.

Ceramic Tile

An economical choice for bathroom and kitchen countertops, ceramic tile that's made locally and incorporates recycled materials is a particularly eco-friendly option. Ceramic tile is impervious to water, heat, and stains, but the grout binding the tiles needs to be sealed regularly to protect against stains, mold, and mildew. If you go with tile, make sure that a complete line of accessories is available, such as bull-nose edges and trim pieces. Also select tile that's rated strong

enough for countertop use so that individual tiles don't break if something heavy is dropped on them.

Plastic Laminate

Made of a thin layer of plastic bonded to particleboard or plywood, plastic laminate counters are more affordable than many other choices and are available in hundreds of patterns and colors. While this type of countertop is stain-resistant and easy to keep clean, it's not very heat-resistant and damage can be difficult if not impossible to repair. Laminate can also be problematic around sinks if water seeps under the surface layer into the wooden core below. For this reason, flush and undermount sinks should not be installed in a laminate countertop. Also make sure the seams stay flush so spills don't penetrate from the surface. To protect your indoor air quality, look for laminate countertops that use no-added formaldehyde plywood or particleboard.

CLOCKWISE FROM LEFT
Pink pigment gives this concrete countertop a softer look. Artist Buddy Rhodes designed it to match the concrete floor tiles below.

Manufacturers like Eleek (shown) and Alkemi use recycled aluminum to create unique countertops.

PaperStone is made of recycled paper combined with a cashew-oil binder. The material is easily routed to create special features, such as this integrated drain board.

End-grain bamboo butcher-block counters can be a sustainable alternative. Colors are generally limited to natural blonde or amber.

Countertops at a glance

Stone and Glass Composites

- **Pros:** Wide range of colors and patterns available; resistant to heat, scratches, and stains.
- **Price:** $$–$$$
- **Installation:** Professional fabrication and installation required.
- **Green issues:** Look for manufacturers that use high amounts of post-consumer recycled glass and porcelain rather than quartz stone; composites made only with concrete and aggregate contain no chemicals but must be sealed, while those made with resin binders contain petrochemical-based materials but don't need to be resealed.

Wood

- **Pros:** Wide variety of species and stains; can be sanded and refinished.
- **Cons:** Does not resist heat or water; must be resealed regularly.

- **Price:** $–$$
- **Installation:** Can be installed by homeowners, but professional fabrication and installation are recommended.
- **Green issues:** Buy FSC-certified, locally grown, or reclaimed wood; use water-based, low-VOC stain and sealant or a natural oil finish.

Bamboo

- **Pros:** Sustainable material with a unique look.
- **Cons:** Color options are limited, as bamboo doesn't take stain well.
- **Price:** $–$$
- **Installation:** Can be installed by homeowners, but professional fabrication and installation are recommended.

- **Green issues:** Not a local product; choose solid bamboo made with formaldehyde-free adhesives, or bamboo veneer attached to an FSC-certified plywood core with no added formaldehyde; use water-based, low-VOC polyurethane sealant or a natural oil finish.

Stainless Steel

- **Pros:** Hard-wearing; resists water, rust, heat, and bacteria.
- **Cons:** Scratches easily; shows fingerprints and water spots.
- **Price:** $$–$$$
- **Installation:** Requires professional fabrication and installation.
- **Green issues:** Combine with a plywood core that has no added formaldehyde; look for recycled stainless steel.

Solid Surface

- **Pros:** Available in hundreds of colors and patterns; can be fabricated into any shape; can include integral sinks; highly durable; scratches can be sanded out.
- **Cons:** Plastic types are made from a petrochemical material and are not recyclable or biodegradable; not very heat-resistant.
- **Price:** $$
- **Installation:** Requires professional fabrication and installation.
- **Green issues:** Choose a solid-surface countertop made of recycled or FSC-certified paper or bamboo fiber with no petrochemical binders.

Concrete

- **Pros:** Can be made in any shape and with integral sinks; wide range of stain colors available.
- **Cons:** Will likely form hairline cracks over time; heavy; must be resealed regularly.
- **Price:** $$–$$$
- **Installation:** Hire an experienced contractor for a poured-in-place counter; slabs require professional fabrication and installation.
- **Green issues:** Include fly ash in custom mixes, or buy preformed slabs that include fly ash and other recycled content; use soy-based stains and low-VOC sealants.

Fiber Cement

- **Pros:** Lighter than poured-in-place concrete; no messy installation in your home; available in a growing number of colors; some include aggregates.
- **Cons:** Must be resealed regularly; will likely form hairline cracks over time.
- **Price:** $–$$$
- **Installation:** Requires professional fabrication and installation.
- **Green issues:** Select manufacturers that use high amounts of fly ash and recycled content; use low-VOC sealants.

Natural Stone

- **Pros:** High-end look; hundreds of colors and patterns available.
- **Cons:** Some types are easy to scratch and must be resealed regularly; heavy.
- **Price:** $–$$$
- **Installation:** Requires professional fabrication and installation.
- **Green issues:** Use a remnant or salvaged piece; choose stone quarried close to home.

Glass

- **Pros:** Stylish and unique; naturally resists heat and stains.
- **Cons:** Can be scratched or cracked; glass tiles have grout to maintain.
- **Price:** $$–$$$
- **Installation:** DIY-friendly; use a white mastic so you won't see it through the tiles; slabs require professional installation.
- **Green issues:** Look for tiles and slabs made of recycled glass.

Ceramic Tile

- **Pros:** Broad range of sizes, shapes, and colors; resists water, heat, and stains.
- **Cons:** Grout can be hard to keep clean and must be resealed regularly.
- **Price:** $–$$
- **Installation:** DIY-friendly.
- **Green issues:** Look for tiles that incorporate recycled materials, or use salvaged or surplus tiles that would otherwise go to waste.

Plastic Laminate

- **Pros:** Available in hundreds of colors and patterns.
- **Cons:** Made from petrochemical-based materials; relatively easy to scratch; stains and scratches cannot be repaired; water exposure will damage substrate.
- **Price:** $–$$
- **Installation:** Can be purchased ready-made or constructed on-site by experienced do-it-yourselfers.
- **Green issues:** Look for recycled plastic and FSC-certified substrates with no added formaldehyde.

ABOVE Made of pressed sunflower hulls, this countertop uses an agricultural waste product and has gorgeous color and depth. But it can be installed only in places that are dry, as water or moisture will cause it to expand.

Saving Water and Energy

Anchored by midsize stainless steel appliances, this small kitchen features salvaged building materials such as the farmhouse sink, the wood beams on the plaster ceiling, and a brick floor.

Whether you have an older, leaky, inefficient house or a new (or newly remodeled), well-insulated home, how you use the house and what appliances and fixtures you put in it have a great impact on how eco-friendly it is.

What do you really need? In recent years, we've seen a lot of kitchens built with two refrigerators, a wine cooler, and a warming oven, as well as bathrooms with soaking tubs and multihead shower systems. Every appliance you add to your home will use gas, electricity, or water, so start by sizing the appliances properly to avoid skyrocketing utility bills in years to come, when natural resources will be more scarce and costly.

Appliances

While using what you have is a stalwart green principle, it does not always apply to appliances. Older appliances often use more water and energy than newer models. Donate inefficient appliances to people for whom they would be an improvement (or recycle them) and seek out Energy Star-certified replacements. The U.S. Department of Energy now requires manufacturers of all major home appliances to have their products tested for energy efficiency. The results of the test are printed on yellow-and-black EnergyGuide labels, which list how much energy the appliance uses and what the annual operating costs may be. Products with EnergyGuide results in the top 25 percent are awarded the Energy Star label. Appliances that have earned an Energy Star rating may cost more than those that have not, but you'll recoup that extra money through lower utility bills down the line. Also, in many areas, there are rebates available for people who buy Energy Star–rated appliances.

REFRIGERATORS are the main energy users in kitchens, so try to keep them down in number and size. Also avoid adding specialized refrigeration units for wine or for cool drinks for the kids upstairs or in the playroom, as each extra unit consumes a large amount of electricity. If you need more refrigeration space, it's better to get a larger main refrigerator than one or two additional smaller ones. Also stay away from through-the-door ice makers and water dispensers, as they require more energy.

ABOVE A wall oven is mounted at eye level so stooping isn't necessary to use it. When you just want to heat something up quickly, the microwave is a more eco-friendly choice.

RIGHT This refrigerator does double duty as a message board, with a chalk panel on top and a cork panel on the bottom.

BELOW Stashing a mini fridge upstairs might be convenient, but it unnecessarily raises your electricity use.

CLOTHES WASHERS that have earned the Energy Star label cut energy and water consumption by more than 40 percent compared with conventional washers. Without a central agitator, they achieve this mainly by rubbing and spinning clothes through a small amount of water and by spinning wet clothes to the point that they need less time in the dryer. Clothes dryers are not Energy Star rated, because the models are all pretty much the same, but you can reduce energy use by line-drying your clothes as much as possible. When contractor Iris Harrell remodeled her home, she created a large laundry room with lots of space to hang and lay clothes out to dry. "Now that we have the space to line-dry, we use the dryer only for towels and sheets," she says.

DISHWASHERS that are Energy Star rated use at least 41 percent less energy than the federal minimum standard, according to the Department of Energy. They also use less water, and the water they do use doesn't need to be as hot. Up your energy savings by running only full loads and letting the dishes air-dry rather than using the unit's drying option. Used properly, an Energy Star–rated dishwasher requires much less water than hand-washing your dishes.

COOKING APPLIANCES, including ranges, ovens, and cooktops, are available in gas or electric models. Gas cooktops use less energy than electric ones, but they do release carbon monoxide, carbon dioxide, and nitrogren dioxide into the air. For this reason, a gas cooktop or range should always have a hood ventilated to the outside of the house. Ovens, whether gas or electric, should be used only when a microwave or toaster oven won't do the job. It takes far more energy to heat up the oven for a frozen burrito than it does to put the item in the microwave for five minutes. Use the oven only for cooking large meals or baking.

TOP LEFT This paneled dishwasher complements the multicolored linoleum floor.

TOP MIDDLE The most energy-efficient way to dry your laundry is with fresh air and sunshine.

TOP RIGHT Front-loading washing machines generally use less water. This one is built into a bank of eco-friendly cabinetry outfitted with a pullout laundry bin.

BOTTOM LEFT Dishwashers configured into two separate drawers save water and energy by letting you run the cleaning cycle one drawer at a time.

BOTTOM RIGHT Surrounded by windows, this electric cooktop set into a concrete countertop doesn't need any additional ventilation.

Fixtures

They are often considered mere finishing touches chosen for convenience or aesthetics, but the fixtures in your home, including toilets, faucets, showerheads, and bathtubs, have a great impact on your water use. Once you buy the most eco-friendly models, do your best to use them responsibly. Don't leave the water running longer than needed, take shorter showers, and consider incorporating gray-water systems (see pages 98–99).

Similar to Energy Star for appliances, there is a federal program sponsored by the Environmental Protection Agency called WaterSense, whose label indicates that a fixture has been certified by independent testing to meet strict water-saving requirements. According to the EPA, the average American uses about 100 gallons of water each day, and at least 36 states anticipate major water shortages by 2013. It is everyone's

responsibility to rein in water use to protect this natural resource, as shortages have a major impact on the environment as well as on food production, farming, and jobs.

TOILETS account for approximately 30 to 40 percent of residential water use, so you will certainly see a difference in your water bill by upgrading to a low-water-use toilet. Replacing old toilets

LEFT Every fixture in the bathroom, from the toilet to the faucets and the showerhead, should be analyzed— and replaced if needed— to ensure that water isn't being wasted.

RIGHT This aluminum soaking tub is surrounded by windows and natural light, which is good for the spirit. But because of the amount of heated water required to fill it, the tub should be an occasional luxury.

should be a high priority in your efforts to make your home more eco-friendly. Currently, federal mandates require that all new toilets use 1.6 gallons of water per flush or less. WaterSense-labeled toilets use 20 percent less water than that, or about 1.28 gallons per flush, and they must also perform well. Dual-flush toilets are becoming a popular way to save water. Push one button and the flush uses about 0.8 gallons for liquids or paper; push another button and it uses up to 1.6 gallons for solid waste.

FAUCETS in the kitchen and bathroom should be equipped with low-flow aerators that reduce the amount of water coming out. You can replace the aerator on older sink faucets that you don't plan to update. Water flow should be reduced to no more than 2 gallons per minute (gpm), though you can find aerators that reduce it to 1 or 1.5 gpm.

SHOWERHEADS can now be found in 1- or 1.6-gpm models that still get the conditioner out of your hair. Aerating showerheads reduce water flow by mixing air with water droplets, but these can cause the water to lose heat. If you like a really hot shower, you'll keep turning up the hot water with an aerating showerhead, which requires more energy. Laminar-flow showerheads use individual streams of water and don't create as much steam or lose heat like aerating ones.

Any new showerhead you buy must meet the federal mandate of no more than 2.5 gpm, but there is currently no law prohibiting people from installing multiple heads and body sprays in one shower, which wastes thousands of gallons of water, requires more energy to heat the extra water, and often necessitates the addition of a tankless water heater or larger water-supply pipes. If you want to be able to share a shower, put the second showerhead on a separate valve so it can be turned off when not needed, and avoid body sprays altogether. There are also showerheads on the market with a thumb valve on the side that allows you to turn off the water while you soap up and turn it back on when you're ready to rinse.

BATHTUBS of standard size may use less water and energy than a shower, depending on the length of the shower. If you have a low-gpm showerhead, you'll use approximately 10 gallons during a four-minute shower. It takes 30 to 50 gallons to fill a bathtub. So if you tend to do your best thinking in the shower, you'll likely use less water soaking in the tub for 20 minutes than you would during a 20-minute shower. Try not to give in to soaking tubs, which quickly deplete standard water heaters, or jetted tubs, which require electricity to run a pump motor.

This eco-friendly bathroom features a reclaimed Douglas fir vanity, handmade ceramic tiles, and a slate floor. It's also plumbed for a gray-water system to reuse water from the sink and shower in the landscape. Unfortunately, the building department would not approve it for use at the time it was built.

Gray Water

This murky-sounding term has been cropping up a lot lately, but what does it mean? Gray water is any water that comes from your bathroom sinks, bathtubs, showers, and clothes washer that can be reused—instead of going down the waste pipe with truly unusable water from the toilet, kitchen sink, and dishwasher. The idea is to get a second use out of water from sources that have not been contaminated with food or human waste, because many things we use water for, such as irrigation and toilet flushing, don't require potable water. The

building codes in some cities don't allow gray water to be collected or reused in any capacity, but a growing number are allowing gray water to be used for irrigation. There are also products on the market that route sink water into the toilet tank so you can avoid using fresh water for that purpose. Check with your local building department to see if these are allowed in your area.

To reuse gray water in the landscape, you'll need to have a second set of pipes that diverts water from select areas in the home. Generally, these pipes will lead to a gravel area in the yard. The gravel filters the water as it makes its way into a buried cistern. Irrigation pipes then pump the gray water into your sprinkler or drip-irrigation system.

For the past seven years, architect Peter Pfeiffer has lived in a house that incorporates many eco-friendly building methods, including gray-water recycling. Based on his experience, Pfeiffer believes the effort and expense involved in setting up a gray-water system may not be worth it. "It's much more effective to install water-saving fixtures and appliances in the home and have a native or low-water-use landscape than it is to become your own water-recycling utility. If you have eco-friendly fixtures, appliances, and landscaping, then the amount of gray water you are able to harvest—about a few hundred gallons a month—may not be worth all the hassle. Because of this, I prefer rainwater collection for irrigation, when needed," Pfeiffer says (see pages 174–175). "Besides, rainwater doesn't stink as much as gray water."

TOP Some feel that training ourselves to use less water in the home is more beneficial than installing gray-water systems.

BOTTOM Choose native plants that don't require much water for your landscape, and, if your area allows it, consider using gray water for irrigation.

ARCHITECT
ERIC COREY FREED ON

Using Gray Water in the House

Ideally, gray water collected from your home could be used in toilets, but in California, we're not allowed to do that without posting signs above the toilet stating that the water is not potable. The reason is that dogs may drink from toilets, which is a valid point, but posting a sign doesn't seem to solve the problem. My dog can't read, anyway. These silly caveats are preventing gray water from being used in toilets, but I'm guessing the code will change in the next 10 years. It has to. We're simply running out of water and need to find ways to reduce and reuse as much as possible."

Ventilation

Panels that match the color and style of the surrounding cabinetry allow the built-in hood to blend in.

An eco-friendly home should have clean air, so keeping rooms well ventilated is important. When you allow fumes to stagnate in a room, you're breathing in toxins. When you let moisture stagnate in a room with no options for escape, that humidity seeps into the walls and promotes mold and mildew growth behind drywall or wallpaper. If large amounts of mold and mildew form behind walls, a home can develop what's referred to as "sick building syndrome." People who live there may become ill without knowing what's causing the problem, because they can't see the mold.

Kitchens

The right hood vent for your kitchen depends on the size of your cooktop or range, how much and what type of cooking you do, and of course your design preferences. If you do little more than boil water for pasta, heat sauces, and steam vegetables, you'll need a less powerful hood vent than if you cook a lot of meat or deep-fry. Even people who rarely cook should install a hood vent, as simply turning on a gas stove to boil water releases carbon monoxide and moisture into the air that should be removed immediately.

Hiding the hood vent in a bank of upper cabinets is the best option for some kitchen designs and is the least expensive choice. Freestanding chimney hoods can make quite a design statement, but the more artistic ones are pricey. If you plan to move the cooktop to an island during a remodel, you'll most likely need to have new ductwork installed. Because the cooktop won't be against a wall, the ductwork may need to travel under the subfloor straight to the nearest exterior wall. Ventilation options for islands include a chimney hood suspended from the ceiling, or a downdraft vent that pops up from behind the burners. Downdraft vents pull grease and moisture from the surfaces of pots and pans and are not as powerful as overhead vents, so they aren't the best choice for people who do a lot of smoky cooking. Commercial hoods have enjoyed a surge in popularity recently but aren't appropriate for residential kitchens, as they suck too much air out of the room. At best, commercial fans depressurize the room; at worst, they can cause backdrafting by pulling exterior air and contaminants down through your chimney and other openings in the house.

ARCHITECT
PETER PFEIFFER ON

Ventilation

When installing an exhaust fan in a kitchen or bathroom, make sure that the ductwork is large enough to allow the air to move efficiently and that it leads directly to the outside of the house with as few twists and as short a run as possible. However, it's important to remember that overexhausting could be bad for indoor air quality and possibly your health, particularly in parts of the country where there's a lot of humidity in the outside air. Overexhausting could mean you are bringing in air from sources that are not healthy—like down the fireplace or water heater flue, or in from the garage. Opening a window to allow enough fresh air into the house to counteract the exhaust fan could bring in more moist air, and that could contribute to a host of other problems, including dust mites and mildew. So take commonsense steps to avoid polluting the house, and then don't leave exhaust fans on longer than necessary."

TOP This refurbished antique stove has a built-in vent at the back that does an adequate job of pulling steam out of the room.

BOTTOM LEFT Modern versions of downdraft vents do better with cooking grease and fumes than the vintage one shown above, but they are still not as powerful as hood vents. The benefit of this one is that it can recess into the countertop when not in use.

BOTTOM RIGHT It's a good idea to have the powerful vent over this gas cooktop to counteract surrounding crosscurrents.

Bathrooms

While an operable window or skylight in a bathroom can help reduce moisture, every bathroom should also have a fan to help prevent damage to surface finishes or even underlying structures due to the daily steam.

The Home Ventilating Institute (HVI) has a certified rating program that tests ventilation products, including bathroom fans, and its symbol on the product packaging certifies that the product moves as much air as it claims to. The HVI recommends that a bathroom fan be capable of exchanging the air in a room at least eight times per hour. Calculate your bathroom's volume by multiplying its length, width, and height. Then multiply the volume by 8 to determine how many cubic inches of air the fan needs to replace each hour. Divide that number by 60 and you'll get the cubic-feet-per-minute, or cfm, rating for your bathroom fan. For example, if the room is 8 feet long by 7 feet wide and has an 8-foot-high ceiling, the equation would be: $8 \times 7 \times 8 \times 8 = 3,584$, which divided by 60 equals 59.73. So you'd need a 60-cfm fan.

Every bathroom should have at least one 50-cfm fan, but if you have a large bathroom with separate areas for the toilet, bath, and shower, each area should have its own 50-cfm fan. Jetted tubs and steam showers require higher-rated fans. Your architect or builder can help you determine the best fan or system for your situation.

Make sure the fan you choose is quiet, or you won't use it. The amount of noise a fan generates is measured in sones. Look for a sone rating of between 0.5 and 1.5. Ideally, you should run the fan for 20 minutes after a shower or bath to clear the room of moist air. Install a timer switch to keep the fan on for only as long as it's needed so you aren't wasting energy or depressurizing the room. There are also humidity-sensing switches that turn fans on and off automatically.

TOP Plenty of operable windows in a bathroom improves airflow and lets natural light in.

MIDDLE Bathrooms with breathable plaster walls and wooden ceiling and wall paneling will do best with plenty of ventilation.

BOTTOM Bathroom fans can have grilles, or they can look like ceiling light fixtures.

OPPOSITE PAGE A reclaimed round ship window provides plenty of ventilation in this stone-walled shower.

Chapter 4

Bedrooms and Nurseries

The rooms we retire to for the night and where our children sleep and grow are critical spaces in an eco-friendly home. Bedrooms should be free of clutter, dust, and offgassing materials. They should be filled with natural light, connected to the outdoors through windows or skylights, and outfitted with furnishings and finishes that will not pollute the air. Most important, the mattress you sleep on and the bedding you surround yourself with should be organic and free of toxins.

Creating a Restful Environment

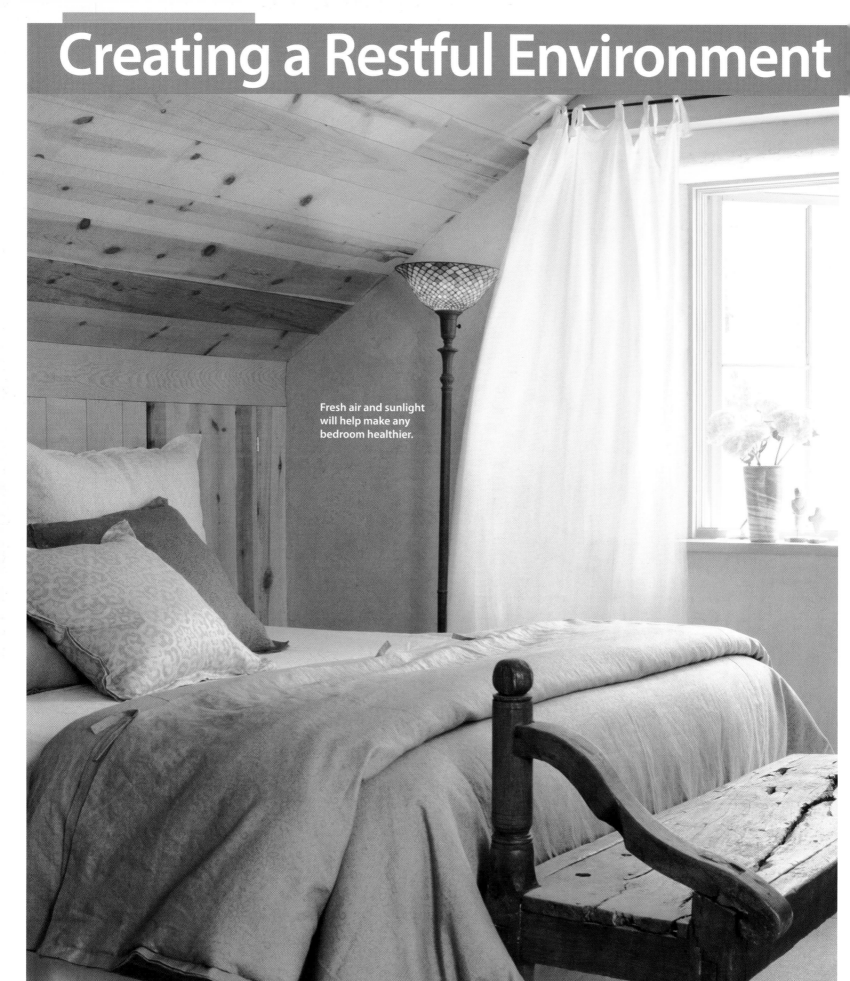

Fresh air and sunlight will help make any bedroom healthier.

TOP LEFT A closet that isn't stuffed to the gills will encourage you to keep things put away instead of strewn across the bedroom.

BOTTOM LEFT In this dual-purpose guest room, a Murphy bed is hidden away in a custom cabinet made with FSC-certified wood and low-VOC finishes.

TOP RIGHT Having a fan over the bed allows you to sleep comfortably without running the air conditioner on hot nights.

BOTTOM RIGHT When the Murphy bed is pulled down, special touches like built-in overhead reading lights and a pullout side shelf make guests feel welcome.

Bedrooms are where we go for rest, relaxation, and rejuvenation, so it's important that they be sanctuaries for our minds and bodies. Many of the experts on our design panel believe that having a healthful bedroom is the most important change you can make in creating a more eco-friendly home.

Keeping your bedroom clean and free of clutter is an important first step. A room with stacks of boxes, papers, and bills is not restful. If your bedroom does double duty as a home office or exercise space, keep things organized and incorporate cabinets with doors that can be closed to hide utility areas of the room. Or use standing fabric panels to block a part of the room that can't be organized easily at the end of each day. Store dirty clothes in a hamper that breathes, and keep your closets uncluttered so you can easily put away clean clothes.

Vacuum or sweep weekly to remove dust and hair that accumulates on the floor, and dust the furniture, baseboards, light fixtures, and the corners of the

ceiling where spiderwebs may collect. Every couple of months, dust the blinds or shutters, or take fabric panels down and shake them outdoors. And, of course, use nontoxic cleaners in the bedroom and throughout the house. Sometimes fumes from cleaning supplies used in an attached bathroom can waft into the bedroom and get absorbed by the bedding and window treatments, so be sure you're using safe cleaners with no scent or scented only with essential oils.

Bedrooms should get some natural light during the day, even if you tend to keep the shades drawn at night. Especially in airtight houses, try to open a window in your bedroom at least once a week to get some fresh air circulating. If your climate is too cold or humid for open windows, consider an air purifier to clear away any impurities. Or get a houseplant that absorbs carbon dioxide and provides clean air (see pages 64–65 for plant recommendations).

CONTRACTOR IRIS HARRELL ON

Temperature and Noise

A healthful bedroom needs fresh air and natural light, and people sleep better when their body temperature is right. We suggest installing whole-house fans that pull air through the home and stay on all night so that the bedroom doesn't get stuffy. If you're building a new house, try not to place any mechanical equipment near the bedroom so people won't be disturbed by air-conditioning motors or refrigerator fans when they're sleeping."

Flooring Choices

Many people prefer carpet in the bedroom, even if they have wood or tile in the rest of the house. It is nice to be able to walk across the bedroom in bare feet without getting cold, but chemicals released from newer standard carpeting or the allergens that get trapped in carpet fibers over the years are high prices to pay for warmer feet.

Homes with radiant-heat systems (see pages 140–141) or in warm climates can do without carpet. If you really need carpet, limit the amount by using well-placed area rugs rather than wall-to-wall coverage. If you're in the market for new carpeting, be sure to get natural, untreated wool carpeting with backing made of jute and rubber, combined with underlayment that does not offgas. If you have carpeting now, consider removing it to improve the air quality in the room. Any amount of carpet needs to be vacuumed at least weekly with a machine outfitted with a HEPA filter. If you suffer from allergies, use small cotton rugs that can be thrown into the washing machine.

Wood, bamboo, cork, and linoleum are all relatively warm and soft underfoot and easy to keep clean. The slight odor of linseed oil in linoleum may bother some people, though, so place a sample in the room as a test before installing. Any new floor should be made of a sustainable material and use formaldehyde-free adhesives. See pages 28–45 for more information about eco-friendly flooring.

Wall Coverings

Choose a color palette for the bedroom that starts with the walls. Earth tones and neutrals create a space conducive to rest. Using no-VOC paint, milk- or plant-based paint, or natural clay wall treatments will ensure that you aren't contributing to unhealthy indoor air quality. If you're drawn to wallpaper, go with a small repeating pattern to cover all four walls, or something more dramatic to cover just one wall. Be sure to buy vinyl-free wallpaper and use no- or low-VOC adhesive (see pages 46–57).

TOP Put a small, washable rug next to the bed so your bare feet won't touch the floor before you get your slippers on.

MIDDLE Stained concrete floors and wood wall paneling give this bedroom a natural, healthy feel.

BOTTOM Crisp blue-and-white walls and bedding are paired with light solid-wood furniture and flooring to create a clean, refreshing space.

OPPOSITE PAGE A floor that doesn't offgas or trap dust is particularly important in a bedroom. This FSC-certified, engineered hickory floor made with formaldehyde-free adhesives and no-VOC stains and sealant holds its own in green and grandeur.

ARCHITECT PAULA BAKER-LAPORTE ON

Electronics in the Bedroom

As a bau-biologist, I'm interested in how radio frequency waves from cell phones, computers, televisions, and other electronic devices create unhealthful living environments. It is particularly important to make the bedroom a neutral electro-climate. Avoid placing your bed against a wall shared with a refrigerator or other motorized equipment because the magnetic fields will penetrate through the wall into your sleep zone. Also replace plug-in alarm clocks with battery-operated models. The best thing to do is to put all of the electrical circuitry in and around the bedroom on a demand switch so you can turn off the surrounding current at night. Try this and you might be surprised how much better you sleep."

Windows

If you're building a new house, your architect will choose the best area for the bedroom so you can wake up to the sun rising and take advantage of natural wind and sun patterns. In a remodel, you don't have this luxury, but you may be able to add a larger window or doors leading to a patio. Consider any possible way of increasing the amount of natural light the bedroom gets, so you don't have to use electric lights during the day. In single-story homes or in top-floor bedrooms, a well-placed skylight can be the difference between a cave-like bedroom and one that is bright and cheerful. Install a skylight not directly over the bed, but close enough that you can get a peek at the stars at night.

Place the bed on a wall that isn't shared with a noisy adjoining room. If that's not possible, consider removing the drywall and adding insulation and soundproofing material so a loud appliance or a flushing toilet doesn't wake you up in the middle of the night. Ideally, place your bed across from a window so you'll have a pretty view when you wake up.

Use natural materials for window treatments in the bedroom, choosing organic fabrics when possible for shades or wood finished with no-VOC stain and sealant for shutters. Avoid blinds made of plastic or fabrics treated with a chemical flame retardant. Give yourself options for light control by layering. Combine sheer curtains that let light in with roll-down shades for when you don't want to wake up with the rising sun. These are also beneficial for temperature control if your bedroom is situated to allow direct sun in summer. Wooden shutters do a good job of blocking the sun as well, and they are easier to keep clean than soft window treatments. You want to avoid dust in the bedroom as much as possible.

TOP LEFT This four-poster bed is perfectly positioned for sunrise views.

BOTTOM LEFT Mounted on the bottom of the windows, these roller shades provide privacy while allowing airflow in the room.

TOP RIGHT Soft Roman shades made of organic cotton fabric frame the garden beyond.

BOTTOM RIGHT Surrounded by windows, you can't help but feel close to nature.

ARCHITECT
MICHELLE KAUFMANN ON

Bedrooms That Connect with Nature

I love incorporating large glass doors that lead from a bedroom to a private garden as a way to wake up and connect with the earth as you start each day. Sometimes we add sliding wooden sun doors in front of the glass that can be adjusted to let in more or less sun at varying times of the year. These are great because they allow you to open the window for cross ventilation but still retain some privacy and sun control."

Mattresses

An eco-friendly
bedroom isn't
complete without
an organic mattress
and bedding.

Perhaps the most important element of a healthful bedroom is the mattress you sleep on. If you currently have a conventional mattress, strongly consider moving it to the guest room, donating it, or recycling it so you can sleep on an organic mattress. Conventional mattresses rely on chemical treatments to do the work that untreated wool does naturally. What makes standard mattresses inexpensive is what makes them harmful.

Highly toxic chemicals with proven negative effects on human health—including PBDEs, boric acid, formaldehyde, toluene diisocyanate, styrene, and butadiene—are commonly used in conventional mattresses. Some of these ingredients are found in foam padding, others are applied as flame retardants, and insecticides are sometimes used to ward off dust mites. Studies have shown that these chemicals actually seep into our bodies while we sleep.

In addition to chemicals, there's the issue of allergens. Dust mites love to live inside petrochemical-based foam or cotton mattresses, and it's their droppings that cause allergy symptoms. Covering a conventional mattress from the start with a dust-mite cover can help prevent airborne triggers. Make sure you buy a cover made of cotton (preferably organic) rather than a synthetic material.

Luckily, there are expanding choices for healthy mattresses on the market, but beware of misleading advertising by companies that may offer one or two natural materials but still spray the entire mattress with chemical flame retardants, for example. Stay away from foam mattresses, even those that say they use soy-based foam. If you like the feel of a "memory foam" bed, try a natural rubber mattress in which at least 95 percent of the rubber comes straight from the serum of the rubber tree and the rest is made up of nontoxic additives needed to pour and bake the rubber, such as sulfur and soaps. The mattress casing should be made of organic cotton and have wool tufting to act as a natural flame retardant. Solid rubber mattresses are a great choice for allergy sufferers, as dust mites are repelled by rubber and wool. Therefore, there's no need to sheathe a natural rubber mattress with a dust-mite cover. You can also find untreated innerspring mattresses made with nontoxic materials such as organic cotton and wool.

PILLOWS AND MATTRESS TOPPERS should be made of eco-friendly materials as well. Have you ever noticed how pillows tend to get heavier over time? That's from accumulated dust, dead skin cells, and the waste of the mites who feed on them. Not a pleasant thought! If you have an old pillow made of synthetic materials, petrochemical foam, or cotton, get rid of it. Replace it with a rubber or wool-filled pillow that naturally resists dust mites. Prefer the loft of cotton pillows? Buy an organic one and keep it covered with an organic cotton barrier cloth to ward off dust mites. And don't forget your throw pillows. Replace synthetic poly-filled ones with those stuffed with organic cotton, organic spun corn fiber, wool, or kapok, and covered in untreated organic fabrics.

Bedding

Just as the chemicals in mattresses will make their way into your body, so will those in the sheets you sleep on. Standard cotton sheets contain pesticides used in growing the cotton, and standard dyes include heavy metals such as lead. Some people prefer wrinkle-free sheets, but just as with any other "foolproof" product, you're taking a hit on health, as the sheets are treated with formaldehyde to keep them flat.

A few years ago, you could find only off-white organic cotton sheets, but today there are more colors and designs using low-impact inks. Many start-up organic-bedding companies are helping to generate a new eco-industry in India, providing fair-trade jobs for people where much of the world's organic cotton is grown.

INTERIOR DESIGNER
KELLY LAPLANTE ON

Organic Bedding

Plan to splurge on an organic mattress and bedding. It's the one place in the house where I always tell my clients to buy something new. And once you have organic bedding, be sure to wash it using nontoxic detergent. There's no point in having organic sheets if you wash them in something that adds harmful chemicals."

Furniture

A solid-wood chest at the foot of the bed holds extra blankets.

Once you've decided to purchase a healthful mattress and bedding, it makes sense to consider the rest of the furniture in the room, starting with the bed frame. Lower-priced bed frames are often made of particleboard or plywood with a wood veneer that's been coated in oil-based finishes. Formaldehyde in the adhesives of pressed-wood products will seep out of the furniture wherever an edge is exposed (veneered furniture is often left unfinished in the back). And the finishes on the wood itself also contain toxins that will offgas over time.

The safest thing to do is to buy solid-wood bed frames, dressers, and cabinets that are either unfinished or finished with a natural hardwax oil or a low-VOC, water-based polyurethane. Solid-wood furniture will cost more, but it will most likely be better made and last longer. A growing number of furniture makers build with local reclaimed wood, which reuses material and results in furniture with a unique patina and sturdy construction. Look for pieces from companies that specifically state that they use no- or low-VOC finishes on their products.

Upholstered furniture such as couches and chairs should be either secondhand (so that offgassing is reduced) or made

ABOVE Push-latch flat-panel cabinets hide books and extra bedding in this clean and modern bedroom.

LEFT Combining vintage pieces with metal and rattan furniture is easier on the wallet than buying solid-wood bedroom furniture.

RIGHT In a creative reuse of salvaged material, this headboard is made of an old door dressed up with crown molding and a fresh coat of no-VOC paint.

ARCHITECT
PAULA BAKER-LAPORTE ON

Maintaining a Healthful Environment

You can spend all of this money and time constructing a nontoxic home and destroy it within five minutes of occupation by bringing in plug-in deodorizers, pesticides, and furniture full of formaldehyde. Homeowners need to be educated that maintenance and furnishings are critical aspects of the health of the building and that what you bring into the home can make or break the environment."

of safe materials such as natural rubber, organic cotton, and wool. A great green idea for the bedroom is to find an old piece of furniture and take it to a local upholstery shop to replace the foam with rubber and cover the piece in organic or untreated fabric.

DECLUTTERING is an important aspect of a healthful bedroom. When you consider the furniture in the room, select pieces that do double duty, such as a storage bench at the foot of the bed that can store seasonal comforters and offer extra seating. If you tend to unload your pockets or purse in the bedroom at the end of the day, put a few baskets on your dresser to keep the contents organized. Surfaces kept free of clutter are much easier to dust.

Nurseries and Kids' Rooms

If you want to add a wool area rug to the nursery, find one that's untreated and has a natural jute-and-rubber backing that won't release harmful chemicals.

TOP Co-sleepers are a great way to keep a newborn close by at night. Be sure your mattress and bedding are also chemical-free if your baby will be sleeping near or in your bed.

BOTTOM LEFT Set up a wooden rocking chair near the window so you and your baby can enjoy the natural light.

BOTTOM RIGHT This changing cart is on wheels so it can be moved out of the way when it's not needed. It's equipped with baskets, buckets, and hanging rods to keep everything organized.

Even people who aren't convinced that they need to make changes in their own bedroom become concerned when it comes to the environment they create for a new baby. For many new parents, reading up on caring for a newborn is what ignites a sense of responsibility for the materials with which we surround ourselves.

Floors and Walls

Before you delve into a design for your new baby's nursery, look at the bones of the room. The developing minds and bodies of babies make them particularly sensitive to the chemicals found in building materials and furnishings. While many people prefer carpet in a nursery because it provides a soft surface for when the baby starts to crawl, carpet traps dust and pollen and is almost impossible to fully clean. Most carpet is made of synthetic material that's treated with stain guards, and these chemicals have even more of an impact on babies. So it's best to remove old carpeting from a nursery altogether. If you add an area rug over hard flooring, make sure it's made of nontoxic materials (see pages 42–43).

Cork is a sustainable and nontoxic option that's soft for crawling babies. Wood floors finished with natural oil or water-based, low-VOC polyurethane are also a good choice. Put washable area rugs over natural rubber antislip mats for added comfort when kids are playing on the floor.

Paint the nursery with no-VOC, milk-based, or plant-based paint (see pages 46–49). Complete any remodeling projects at least a month before the baby arrives, then flush out the room with fresh air. As in the rest of the house, you can take great care in choosing the materials to finish the space, but then add things that will ruin the indoor air quality. It's tough to do, but try not to buy plastic toys or stuffed animals treated with flame retardants.

ARCHITECT
ERIC COREY FREED ON

Light Control

Babies sleep during the day, so you need to have a way to keep natural light out. Look for vinyl-free blinds or bare wooden shutters that can be finished with no-VOC stains and sealants. If you choose soft window coverings, make sure they're made of an untreated fabric that can be washed regularly to keep dust out of the nursery."

A Safe Place to Sleep

LEFT Invest in an organic crib mattress and bedding so your new baby isn't breathing in harmful chemicals while sleeping.

RIGHT Keep soft toys that are treated with flame retardants and stuffed with synthetic materials out of the house. You can now find alternatives made of untreated fabrics that are filled with organic cotton, wool, or spun corn fiber.

Babies spend a lot of time sleeping, so it's especially important to surround them with nontoxic materials in their cribs. Like adults' mattresses (see pages 112–113), conventional crib mattresses are treated with hormone-disrupting chemicals that are particularly toxic to babies. Crib mattresses made of synthetic materials and treated with flame retardants are quite reasonably priced, so you may experience a bit of sticker shock when you shop for organic crib mattresses that use wool as a natural flame retardant.

If at all possible, find a way to buy an organic crib mattress. One option may be to go in on one with your siblings or friends who will be having babies of their own after your child grows out of the crib. Natural rubber mattresses in particular are sturdy enough to be used for multiple babies over many years. Instead of a plastic cover, protect the mattress from accidents with a natural wool moisture-barrier cloth that can be washed and air-dried. There are also many adorable options for organic crib bedding today, so you don't have to buy chemically treated sheets, bumpers, and skirts to have colorful patterns.

Cribs and Furniture

Many parents want to keep costs down when outfitting a nursery, because the period when a crib and changing table are needed is so short.

If you have a tight budget, the healthiest way to furnish the nursery is not with inexpensive pressed-wood furniture but with secondhand cribs and dressers. This furniture will have already offgassed for the most part and can be refinished with a fresh coat of no-VOC paint.

Interior designer Kelly LaPlante loves to find antique furniture for her high-end nurseries. "When we choose antique furniture, first we make sure it's still sturdy enough to use, and then we seal the piece with a coat of high-gloss Safecoat Polyureseal to protect the child from any lead-based paint that may have been used in the past," LaPlante says. "Parents need to inspect these pieces regularly to make sure

there are no cracks or dings that need to be resealed."

If you prefer and can afford new furniture in the nursery, choose FSC-certified solid-wood furniture finished with no-VOC paint or sealant. If the nursery furniture you buy smells bad, or "new," then there are chemicals offgassing. "We bought a dresser for our daughter that smelled so bad we had to line the drawers with baking soda to absorb the formaldehyde," says new father Eric Corey Freed. "The baking soda helped, but it didn't eliminate it. Try to buy the nursery furniture a couple of months in advance so that, if it does smell, you can let it offgas outdoors or in the garage for a while before bringing it into the nursery."

LEFT An old potting bench is given new life as a changing table. If you're planning to make use of a vintage crib or high chair, be aware that they may not meet modern safety guidelines.

RIGHT The small compartments in this vintage sewing table are perfect for storing pacifiers and booties.

Cork flooring in mottled, reddish tones transitions beautifully to the redwood tree mural created with no-VOC paints in this sunny playroom.

Kids' Rooms

Your carefully planned and protected
nursery will soon give way to a child's
room that's much harder to control. The
right furniture and an organized closet
will keep things from becoming unruly
and make it easier for your child to learn
to clean up.

Keep the room healthful by instituting
a "no shoes" rule so that pesticides and
pollen aren't tracked in, and remove the
clothes that have been rolled around in
outdoors before your child jumps into
bed. Once your baby is too big for the
crib, make a long-term investment in an
organic mattress that will last through
college. If your child suffers from asthma
or allergies, remove all carpeting or area
rugs from the room and keep soft toys
out as well.

ABOVE A vintage
dresser is paired with
a custom-built bunk
bed in this bright
kids' room.

RIGHT It's a tall order,
but try to keep plastic
toys out of the
bedroom in favor
of wooden toys that
meet European safety
standards for finishes.

Chapter 5

Light and Comfort

An eco-friendly home should have an energy-efficient lighting plan, windows that help retain heated and cooled air, well-positioned windows and skylights to let in the right amount of sunlight, a low-energy and high-efficiency heating system, and the appropriate amount of airflow. It all starts with a well-sited home that takes advantage of natural breezes and sun patterns. If you're improving an existing home rather than building a new one, consider using more efficient light bulbs and window treatments, adding windows or skylights, and incorporating passive solar heating and cooling principles.

Lighting

Warm lighting combined with a roaring fire creates a welcoming glow.

When you're building a new house or embarking on a major remodel, you can design it so that natural light streaming through windows and skylights is all you'll need to function inside the house when the sun is up. But many of us live in houses that were not designed with this concept in mind, so electric lights are necessary during most of the day. Whichever camp you fall into, this section will inform you of the different choices for light bulbs and fixtures and how you can make your existing lighting plan more energy efficient.

Don't underestimate the importance of a well-thought-out lighting plan. "Feeling good in your home has a lot to do with lighting," says contractor Iris Harrell. "When budgets get tight, people tend to want to save on the lighting, but doing this will compromise the way the house feels and functions."

The Demise of Incandescent Bulbs

When Thomas Edison unveiled the first commercially viable incandescent light bulb in 1879, it was a life-changing moment in history. But it is now time to retire this technology in favor of more energy-efficient models. While the light quality of incandescents is generally far preferred by designers and homeowners, the amount of electricity needed to run them and the fact that 90 percent of the energy they burn is wasted are making a large impact on the environment. So large, in fact, that the U.S. government passed an energy bill in 2007 that includes a phaseout of incandescent bulbs, starting with the 100-watt bulb in 2012 and ending with the 40-watt bulb in 2014. Australia was the first country to ban incandescents, and its bulbs will be phased out by 2010.

Compact Fluorescent Lamps

We all know that replacing incandescent bulbs with compact fluorescent lamps (CFLs) will save energy, but too few people are making the switch. In 2008, CFLs accounted for just 20 percent of all light bulbs sold. Common complaints are that the light output isn't warm enough, that the bulbs are too expensive, that they don't fit in some fixtures, and that they contain mercury. But over the past several years, manufacturers have made great strides in all of these areas.

CFLs use roughly one-third as much electricity as incandescent bulbs of the same wattage, and they generate much less heat, which means you don't have to air-condition a space to counteract the heat coming off the bulbs. They are available in a much wider variety of sizes and wattages than they used to be, and they can screw into most existing fixtures. Dimmable CFLs were once hard to find but are now making their way into the marketplace. And the fact that CFLs can last up to 10 times as long as incandescent bulbs makes up for the higher price.

The mercury contained in one CFL is 5 milligrams or less, an amount equal in size to the tip of a pen. It doesn't make sense to avoid CFLs just because they contain mercury, as the increased energy consumption of incandescent bulbs releases far more mercury into the environment when coal is burned to generate that electricity. While manufacturers have significantly lowered the amount of mercury in CFLs over the past decade, there is still enough to qualify the bulbs as toxic waste. Most states do not currently outlaw throwing CFLs into the regular trash, but more communities are starting to encourage homeowners to recycle them. It's likely that your local home improvement center will recycle your old CFLs. If not, call your local waste-management facility to ask where you can take your bulbs to dispose of them safely.

TOP Compact fluorescent bulbs illuminate a covered outdoor room.

BOTTOM LEFT Incandescent bulbs are not energy efficient and will be phased out in coming years.

BOTTOM RIGHT Compact fluorescent bulbs are available in various sizes, wattages, and color tones.

Light-Emitting Diodes

While the high price of light-emitting diodes is prohibitive enough to keep them in the specialty category for now, they are currently the only energy-efficient lighting option that does not rely on mercury vapor. LEDs can last four times as long as CFLs, and they stay cool to the touch.

Architect Eric Corey Freed currently uses LEDs when he has very specific color or temperature requirements, or as an accessory to other light sources. He plans to use them more when they come down in price. "LEDs are a good choice when you can't access the bulb easily, because they last so long you might never have to change them. For example, I use them in glass blocks embedded in outdoor stairways or patios because you can just put them in and forget about them," he says.

Halogens

Most often used as accent lighting, halogens produce a whiter and brighter beam than other bulbs. The main downside to halogens is the heat they emit, which is significant enough that they must be used in fixtures made specifically for them. If you find yourself drawn to low-voltage pendants or downlights requiring halogen bulbs, try to minimize how many you use.

TOP LEFT LEDs are used in under-cabinet lighting because they provide a sharp, focused beam without heating up the surrounding cabinetry.

BOTTOM LEFT Halogen spotlights on tracks provide task lighting in this kitchen.

TOP RIGHT LED bulbs stay cool enough to use with a shade constructed of rice paper.

BOTTOM RIGHT Halogen bulbs require fixtures that are designed for them.

ARCHITECT
PETER PFEIFFER ON

Working with CFLs

There have been great advances in LEDs, but without a doubt, fluorescent is still king. You might get 10 to 15 percent more total fixture efficiency out of an LED system, but right now it will cost you three to five times as much money, and you don't have as many choices in the color tones of the lamps. With fluorescents, a 3,500K bulb is just about white enough for white light. If you want something warmer, choose a 3,000K or 2,800K bulb, which will give off light quality similar to that of an incandescent. With fluorescents, we can light a kitchen with 300 to 350 watts. A typical high-end kitchen using incandescents uses about 1,500 watts, or even more. When you consider that every watt equals 3.4 BTUs of heat, you'll save a fair amount of money on air-conditioning with fluorescents."

TOP LEFT Architect Michelle Kaufmann designed this unique fixture, which shoots light up through a glass tube that can hold decorations such as flowers or stones. It also shoots light down along the wall. The fixture is outfitted with a 13-watt CFL.

TOP RIGHT Designed by a San Francisco company, the lite2go fixture uses the product packaging as the lampshade. Inside what will become the shade are a CFL bulb and a cord. Detailed instructions show you how to build your own lamp, and all the components are either biodegradable or recyclable.

BOTTOM LEFT The warm glow of the Moso pendant, designed by Brian Schmitt, is created from a CFL bulb shining through bamboo veneer panels. Available in end-grain and vertical-grain bamboo, the pendants are made without adhesives and shipped flat to minimize packaging.

BOTTOM RIGHT Designer Helen Gifford thought of a clever way to reuse old incandescent light bulbs without making them the light source. Her delicate Eco-Urchin pendants are made in New York.

Green Lighting Fixtures

Once you've decided to swap out your incandescent light bulbs for CFLs, you might also take a look at the growing number of options for eco-friendly fixtures. Creative lighting designers are thinking of new ways to address everything from the materials the fixtures are made of to how they are packaged and shipped. Before buying something new, though, try to find a suitable fixture at your local salvage yard and have it rewired. When you're in the market for a new fixture, give preference to those made of eco-friendly materials, such as bamboo, FSC-certified wood, and recycled glass.

The Furrow pendant, by Propellor Design, is a bamboo box decorated with holes that allow light from a CFL bulb to shine through.

Daylighting Options

When you walk into a house full of windows and natural light, you will feel a positive energy radiating from it. The inhabitants of that house will be happier and healthier because they are connected to nature and are reaping the benefits of the mood-changing power of sunlight. In a well-designed and well-sited home, electric lights are used little if at all when the sun is up.

"Daylighting doesn't mean adding as much natural light as possible. Rather, it's the quality of light that you're after," says architect Eric Corey Freed. "It means light from more than one direction. If you have a shoebox loft with one wall that's floor-to-ceiling glass, you'll have blinding light. It's about having an understanding of how the winter versus the summer sun comes in and designing around that. For example, winter sun is lower than summer sun, so that determines the configuration of indoor window treatments."

Windows

If you are building a new house or tearing your current house down to the studs, you can work with an architect on placing windows for optimal views, sunlight, and natural breezes. There is an art to this process, and when it's done correctly, the house will be brighter and more energy efficient. For people who are not in this position, there are still opportunities to bring in more natural light. It may be possible to add windows to existing walls or to install skylights (see pages 132–133).

Windows should be double-paned, weather-stripped, and caulked for minimal air transfer when closed. Single-pane or poorly installed windows can let up to 25 percent of your inside heated or cooled air out of the house, wasting the energy it took to create it. Go to any salvage yard and you will see hundreds of old single-pane windows that have been replaced with newer models. It may seem quicker and easier to replace the windows in this way, but the most eco-friendly option is to have old windows refurbished. Especially in a home whose windows lend it architectural character, it's worth looking into how they can be repaired or upgraded. Find a window restorer who will add weather-stripping, install new sash locks for a tighter seal, and add insulation in the weight pockets, over the header, and under the sill of a double-hung window. You can also have new jamb liners installed to seal the area between the sash and the jamb if necessary. These improvements should stop draftiness, and you can then add storm windows if your climate requires them or to solve condensation problems. However, if your current windows are rotted, you will have to replace them. Choose Energy Star–rated windows and get them installed by an expert who will make sure there are no leaks of water or air.

ARCHITECT
MATT ELLIOTT ON

Windows in Cold Climates

It may be even more important for people in cold climates to feel connected to the outdoors, so I try to design as many windows into a house as I can justify. Most are put on the south side of the house, but some are on the north to balance out the light and provide cross-ventilation. We usually install double-pane, insulated glass with low-e coatings, but occasionally we'll do triple-pane windows. With the right type of glass and the right window placement, you can actually end up with an energy gain."

OPPOSITE PAGE A bank of windows on the second story of this house brings light in and moves hot air out. Skylights in the patio roof allow light into first-floor windows as well.

TOP These sliding glass doors are paired with shoji screens to diffuse the light when the summer sun shines straight into the living room.

BOTTOM LEFT Placing windows high on a wall allows light to stream in without sacrificing privacy.

BOTTOM RIGHT Try to refurbish old wooden windows to make them more energy efficient. Replace them only if you have to.

Skylights

By increasing natural light and making a room feel larger, skylights can give you a big bang for your remodeling buck. The trick is to place and size them appropriately; otherwise, you'll add unwanted heat. Consider how your house is positioned on the site, the size of the room, and the colors and reflective surfaces in the room before committing to the skylight's size and location. When your design calls for a large skylight, include a remotely controlled shade to block the sunlight on hot days.

OPERABLE SKYLIGHTS give you another ventilation option high up in a room, where the heat naturally accumulates. Some can be opened with an extension pole, while others can be wired for remote control. There are also particularly high-tech models with rain sensors that close automatically at the first sign of a sprinkle.

TUBULAR SKYLIGHTS bring daylight into areas of the house where it wouldn't normally be possible, such as in a hallway with no exterior access. A rooftop dome catches sunlight and bounces it down a reflective tube into an interior diffuser that looks a lot like an electric ceiling light. The tubes can make turns to reach the right location in your ceiling without losing any sunlight. Some are equipped with CFLs so they can continue to provide light at night.

Translucent Walls

Aside from windows and skylights, there are creative and architecturally interesting ways to add natural light to a room. Glass blocks can be used instead of gypsum board and siding in portions of a wall to allow light into the room, and they have enough distortion that you don't need to cover them with window treatments. Their watery appearance makes them a popular addition in showers and tub surrounds. Resin panels can be integrated in interior doors and walls so that natural light coming from a window in one room can be transferred to an interior room or hallway.

TOP Resin panels with bamboo stalks obscure the dishes in this upper cabinet while also allowing natural light into the kitchen, thanks to a window strategically placed on the exterior wall behind the cabinet.

MIDDLE A skylight hidden in a channel above this vanity sink provides enough sunlight that the hanging fixture remains off during the day.

BOTTOM Translucent ribbed panels form an interior wall that passes natural light from the bedroom to the living space.

OPPOSITE PAGE This skylight works in harmony with sliding glass doors to brighten up a kitchen with a dark hardwood floor.

ARCHITECT
MICHELLE KAUFMANN ON

Designing with Natural Light

There's so much you can do to use less. Really study the light patterns in remodels so you can place windows and skylights in the right spots to maximize light and cross-ventilation. Wash the walls with natural light from high windows and skylights, and the floors with light streaming in through glass doors. In interior spaces that have no exterior walls, put in skylights as a way to sculpt natural light."

Window Treatments

The hardwood floor, wooden blinds, and ceiling beams are all finished with low-VOC stain and sealant.

TOP Make your own window valance and curtains from colorful vintage fabric.

LEFT Window treatment hardware can be a background player or the star of the show.

RIGHT These thick silk draperies hanging on a bamboo rod reduce heat loss on cold days.

INTERIOR DESIGNER
KELLY LAPLANTE ON

Eco-Friendly Window Treatments

A lot of my clients love to go to chain decorating stores for a quick window treatment fix. There are starting to be some eco-friendly off-the-shelf options, but most of the time I rely on custom shades and drapes so I can use organic fabrics in the colors and patterns I want. If you need something fast and you can't find any simple organic solutions, buy linen drapery instead of cotton, because it's grown without pesticides for flax."

Besides contributing to the design and coziness of a room, window treatments help minimize heat transfer from windows. Drapes, blinds, shutters, and shades can all block sunlight from heating up the house on hot days and keep warm or cool air from escaping through leaky windows. Some materials do a better job than others. If you live in a cold climate, look for window coverings whose insulating qualities are advertised.

Eco-friendly fabrics such as organic cotton and hemp are available in a growing number of pretty colors and patterns for custom window treatments. Look for shutters made of FSC-certified hardwood, and finish them with no- or low-VOC stains and sealants. Avoid plastic shutters and blinds, as well as polyester fabrics that won't biodegrade. Woven shades made of bamboo, reeds, and grasses are another green option, as long as they aren't treated with oil-based finishes that will offgas.

Air Movement and Heat

The main hallway of this home acts as a thermal chimney, leading hot air out of the space. The exterior walls were constructed with concrete masonry units, so the house has a lot of thermal mass.

All of the architects on our design panel discussed the importance of moving air through a home. Some prefer to incorporate thermal chimneys, while others combine air movement as part of a heating and cooling system. There are several eco-friendly ways to efficiently heat a home, including geothermal, heat pumps, radiant-heat systems, and forced air. While a technical explanation of each type is beyond the scope of this book, the following pages will get you thinking about how an energy-efficient home is built to work with its heating and cooling system rather than against it. Speak to your architect or builder about the options available for your new home or remodel, and make sure that person considers the site and weather conditions on your property in determining the best solution.

Low-Energy Options

Opening the windows for occasional cross-ventilation and installing ceiling fans in bedrooms so you don't need air-conditioning at night are two simple ways to maintain the right temperature and airflow in your house. But sometimes you need something more.

WHOLE-HOUSE FANS are an inexpensive way to keep a house cool in certain climates, especially if you buy a solar-powered model. The fan should be installed at the home's highest point. During the day, especially if your house has little to no shade from surrounding mature trees, it becomes hotter as the hours pass. By early evening, it may be hotter inside the house than outside. In late afternoon, open the windows that are farthest from the whole-house fan to flush hot air out of the house and bring cooler air in. If you use a whole-house fan without opening a window, it can result in depressurization or backdraft, bringing in air you don't want moving through the house, from the chimney or hood vent, for example. Climates with high levels of humidity aren't good candidates for whole-house fans, as bringing in outside air can cause other problems (see page 101).

THERMAL CHIMNEYS are another way to carry hot air out of a house. Generally, these are designed in the main hallway or at a staircase as a very high area with operable windows at the top. Typically, thermal chimneys work in conjunction with cool-air inlet vents placed on the side of the house that receives the prevailing cool summer breezes. Hot air is pulled upward, and the windows let it out and also make the hallway or stairwell brighter.

When you set up air to move through a house evenly, closed bedroom doors can ruin the effect. Architect Peter Pfeiffer suggests installing passive return air vents or jumper ducts between the bedrooms and hallway. "Without those, the more air you pump into that room with the door closed, the more the rest of the house goes into negative pressure, possibly pulling outside air in through the chimney or other places you don't want," Pfeiffer says.

ARCHITECT
PAULA BAKER-LAPORTE ON

Working with Your Climate

From a building-biology standpoint, if you have good outdoor air where you live, then you should have an outside air-intake duct that feeds through your HVAC system. Recirculated HVAC air can be too dry in the winter in some climates. If you have a home with a lot of thermal mass, like an adobe home, you can open a window for fresh air without having the temperature drop, but a regular home will get colder if outside air is brought in this way. So you have to figure out how to use the climate you live in to your best advantage."

Passive Heating and Cooling

Using your site effectively can make the difference between a house that relies on year-round gas or electric heating and air-conditioning and one that needs only supplemental heating and cooling, if any at all. When sunlight shines through south-facing glass and hits a surface with thermal mass inside the house (such as concrete, stone, or brick), the material absorbs and later releases the heat into the surrounding air. The trick is to size and place your windows and skylights appropriately, and add correctly sized overhangs or shading, to get the right amount of heat. If the south-facing wall has windows that equal more than 12 percent of the square footage of the room's floor, you might be bringing in too much heat. An experienced architect can help determine the right mix for your

LEFT Designed by architect Cliff May, this house has walls made of adobe bricks that keep the interior cool enough to never need air-conditioning. The skylight above the living room was added during a recent remodel to let in more sunlight, increasing the passive solar properties of the concrete aggregate floor.

particular climate. And you don't have to be building a new house to do this. It's possible to increase passive heating and cooling during a remodel.

Just as you can welcome the sun to heat up materials with thermal mass, you can block out the sun to allow the same materials to maintain the ambient temperature of the earth. Concrete, stone, and tile floors stay naturally cool if they aren't heated up by the sun or radiant-heat systems, and that coolness radiates into the house and can reduce or eliminate the need for air-conditioning.

Homes built or remodeled with passive heating and cooling in mind have deep roof overhangs. While standard roof overhangs are 1 to 2 feet deep, overhangs of 6 feet or more shade windows from the sun during the hottest part of the day. Trellises built against the house can serve the same purpose. Architect Michelle Kaufmann prefers operable trellises with rotating louvers. The louvers can be more vertical in winter to allow sunlight in, and more horizontal in summer when you need more shade. "We try not to have windows face west unless it's a great view, in which case we add large roof overhangs," Kaufmann says. "Our Breezehouse

modular home uses stone flooring in some of the main living spaces to gather heat during the day and release it at night when you'd normally need to turn on a heater."

Architect Paula Baker-Laporte is also a big believer in passive heating and cooling. "In our New Mexico climate, it's really a no-brainer," she says. "It should be used in every house, but unfortunately you don't see much of it in standard new home construction."

"Techno-toys like solar water heaters and solar panels are the icing on the cake but are not as effective as doing a climate-sensitive design," says architect Peter Pfeiffer. "Orienting a house correctly is one of the most important things you can do to save energy in most climates. We maximize north- and south-facing windows and make sure we have properly sized roof overhangs by performing sun-angle calculations that are based on the climate we're building in."

Forced-Air Heating

Heating your home with a gas furnace can be done well but is often not an efficient solution if your furnace isn't sized correctly for your home or if your ducts are leaky. Too few contractors take the time to do load calculations to ensure that a furnace is powerful enough to heat a home but is not overly powerful. Poorly installed ductwork can leak heated or cooled air, causing negative pressure in the house and possibly pulling carbon monoxide out of the gas appliances in your home. Good contractors use duct mastic rather than tape on all duct joints to prevent these problems.

Radiant Heat

Radiant heat does not use any ductwork to move warm air through the house. Instead, the heat comes from tubes buried in a concrete subfloor or installed under or over a wood subfloor (but beneath the finished floor). That heat naturally rises into the living space. In hydronic radiant-heat systems, the

tubes are heated with water from a boiler or water heater that's powered by gas, electricity, or solar energy. There are also radiant-heat mats that use electrical wires rather than water to warm a space.

"Seventy-five percent of the homes our firm builds have hydronic radiant-heat systems," says architect Matt Elliott. "Sometimes we use radiant in one part of the house and a baseboard heat system in another part of the house to keep costs down. In rooms that have more of a temperature swing, the baseboard system responds a bit quicker than radiant." Both the radiant system and the baseboard heater can run off the same boiler. With this hybrid system, energy is saved because the radiant system can be kept at a relatively low temperature all the time and the baseboard heat system can be turned on for quicker heating when needed.

Architect Eric Corey Freed also likes hybrid systems that include radiant heat. "For rooms that you want to heat all day long during the winter, hydronic radiant systems make sense. But for rooms used once a day, the cost of running the system can be too high. That's why we like to install electric heat mats in bathrooms and other spaces

that are used infrequently," Freed says. When homeowners generate their own electricity with solar panels, an electric mat system is also cost-effective. "Ultimately, this way of combining systems is cheaper to run and uses less energy. It also reduces the size of the hydronic system, as the boiler need not be as large," he says.

Home Performance Testing

More and more contractors and consultants offer home performance testing. The tests determine how airtight your home and ductwork are. They can also tell you how big a factor any old single-pane windows may be in the energy efficiency of your home, how much you could save if you used more efficient lighting and appliances, and whether your home has the proper amount of insulation. A home performance test can cost hundreds of dollars, but if leaks are fixed, you will quickly recoup that money through lower utility bills. Some companies will apply the performance test fee to any work you hire them to do to fix a problem that the evaluation revealed.

LEFT A metal roof deflects heat, while deep overhangs reduce the amount of sunlight coming into the house. When homes are designed like this, heating and air-conditioning can be used supplementally, if at all.

RIGHT This home uses passive solar heating and cooling techniques and has hydronic radiant heat built into the concrete floor. To help move air, windows are placed low and high on the walls. Cool breezes come into the house through the low windows, and hot air is pulled out of the high windows.

Fireplaces

Surrounded by a built-in shelving unit, this gas insert blows enough heat into the room to be the only heat source needed on most days.

Nothing makes a home as cozy as a roaring fire, but in many parts of the country, you can't burn wood on certain days, or at all, because of the air pollution it creates. Standard wood-burning fireplaces are also an inefficient way to heat a space. However, there are several eco-friendly fireplace options that provide warmth and romance.

Gas Inserts

Switch from wood burning to gas with an insert that fits inside your current fireplace. You won't contribute to air pollution, and you'll have a more efficient space heater. Plus, less air will leak through your chimney because of loose-fitting flue dampers. Contractor Iris Harrell had gas inserts with blowers installed in her home. "The unit continues to emit heat even when the fire is turned off, warming up the room enough that we can turn off our forced-air heater and save energy that way," she says.

Woodstoves

In some regions, chopped wood is abundant and inexpensive, which makes a high-efficiency woodstove more cost-effective than a gas-powered unit. Look for models that include a convection

ARCHITECT
MATT ELLIOTT ON

Woodstoves

In Maine, wood-burning fireplaces are allowed, so most of our clients want them. We do try to incorporate woodstoves, however, because they are more efficient than standard fireplaces. Always make sure fireplaces have an outdoor air intake, as well as glass doors to seal off the fire. Those two elements will ensure that you're not losing a lot of energy. If you don't have an outdoor air intake, you'll be drawing heated air into the fire and up through the chimney, wasting air that you paid to heat."

system for moving heat through the room, and for those that produce low smoke emissions.

Masonry Heaters

This is another wood-burning option, but the wood is burned at a very high heat and radiates into the room through a stone surround. Because stone is such a high-mass object, it absorbs heat and releases it slowly, heating up a room without becoming too hot to touch. Architect Paula Baker-Laporte encourages her clients to use masonry heaters. "They don't have the same pollution issues as a typical wood-burning fireplace. In fact, you don't see smoke coming out of the chimney at all, just wavy air. Because of their weight, masonry heaters do need a proper foundation but can be incorporated in a remodel," she says.

TOP LEFT EcoSmart fireplaces look like works of art and can be installed anywhere, as they don't need a flue or a utility connection. They are fueled by denatured ethanol, which is a renewable resource and doesn't pollute the air.

TOP RIGHT Woodstoves are available in sleek, modern styles like this, and in old-fashioned designs that look at home in a rustic cabin.

BOTTOM Tulikivi masonry heaters use soapstone to absorb and release heat from the wood-burning fire. They come in various sizes and designs.

Chapter 6

Exteriors

Now that we've covered the inside of the house, step outside and see how you can make more eco-friendly choices in your front and back yards. This chapter discusses sustainable options for hardscaping and encourages you to collect rainwater, create low-water landscapes, and try growing some of your own fruits and vegetables. As for the bones of the house itself, there are many ways to build structures with energy-efficient and recycled material. We'll go over options for exterior walls and roofing, and we'll also discuss green roofs and solar panels, so you can decide if they are right for you.

Exterior Walls and Finishes

When you're building a new home or adding on to your current one, there are many eco-friendly structural and finish choices to consider. The following pages summarize the available options so you can find a builder who is familiar with the method you're interested in.

Wood Framing

Approximately 90 percent of homes in the United States are made of wood. Done correctly, a stick-framed home can be constructed in an energy-efficient way; but all too often, advanced framing methods are not adhered to and you end up with a house that leaks air and wastes a lot of material. The other concern with stick-framed homes is how much raw lumber is used. Today there are options for FSC-certified framing lumber, which generally costs only about 5 percent more, and you can find reclaimed wood for many framing needs. Builders are also replacing solid wood with engineered wood where they can, using 50 percent less wood to achieve the same strength. However, most engineered wood contains formaldehyde-based adhesives. If your builder can use engineered wood framing, try to find local sources that sell versions with no added formaldehyde.

Steel Framing

Using steel instead of wood to frame a house is an eco-friendly choice for many reasons. The material is strong and fire-resistant, termites aren't an issue, the framing won't rot if exposed to water, the material is recyclable, and of course no trees are cut down to make it. The downside is that metal is a highly conductive material and will transfer heat into the house if used to frame exterior walls, resulting in the need for more air-conditioning in some climates. You can greatly reduce heat transfer by attaching rigid insulation to the exterior side of the framing, or you can limit steel to interior walls.

Steel-framed homes can be covered up with siding so you'd never know what's underneath. Or they can be left exposed, as shown in this clean, modern example.

RIGHT If you want a wood-framed home, use as much FSC-certified and reclaimed material as possible.

Structural Insulated Panels

This relative newcomer to home construction is beginning to catch on because it creates a tight envelope and greatly reduces material waste as the walls are assembled off-site. Structural insulated panels (SIPs) generally consist of two pieces of oriented-strand board (OSB) or metal with an insulating foam core sandwiched between them. Because of the expanded polystyrene foam and engineered wood, some offgassing is involved, but the material creates highly energy-efficient homes. The panels vary in thickness and are cut to the size you need. SIPs can function on their own as load-bearing walls or as exterior panels on a stick- or steel-framed house. Once siding is installed, you would never know a SIP house from one that was built traditionally.

Concrete Options

Insulated concrete forms (ICFs) are polystyrene blocks that are easy to cut and stack around rebar. Once the structure is formed, concrete is poured into the blocks, creating a wall with high insulation value, low air infiltration, a good track record of withstanding high winds and fires, and low noise transmission. As with steel-framed homes, you don't have to worry about insects or rot; but unlike steel, ICFs have a high thermal mass, so they absorb and slowly release heat instead of quickly transferring it inside. This thermal mass creates a house that is cool during hot days and warms up as the sun goes down, when you might otherwise need to supplement with a heating system.

Common in Europe and Asia but only recently introduced in the United States, autoclaved aerated concrete (AAC) is another concrete-based structural building component that shares similar advantages with ICFs, but it does not include any polystyrene foam and is easier to build with. AAC is made of portland cement mixed with lime, silica sand or recycled fly ash, water, and aluminum powder. The reaction between the aluminum and the concrete causes small hydrogen bubbles to form that expand the concrete, making it lighter than traditional poured concrete. The blocks are then steam-heated and cut to various sizes to construct floors, walls, and roofs. The cost is comparable to that of standard concrete masonry units (CMUs). Although walls are constructed similarly for both materials, the work goes faster and the shipping costs are lower with AAC because the material is lighter.

OPPOSITE PAGE Structural insulated panels (SIPs) form the walls of this house and are covered in fiber-cement siding fixed between strips of aluminum. Note the deep roof overhang, which helps keep the house cool.

TOP LEFT SIPs arrive at the job site on a palette, precut and ready to assemble.

TOP RIGHT Erecting the SIP walls takes significantly less time than traditional stick-built framing.

BOTTOM Autoclaved aerated concrete blocks create structures that are energy efficient and quiet.

LEFT Sprayed-earth construction, or PISE, created this textural exterior wall.

BOTTOM Just inside the front door, an area of wall plaster was left unfinished to highlight the home's adobe construction.

OPPOSITE PAGE This rammed-earth house has the look of a French chateau that has stood for centuries, even though it is only a few years old.

Rammed Earth

This centuries-old construction method is eco-friendly but labor-intensive. Rammed-earth walls are made of soil with the proper ratio of sand and clay mixed with water. A temporary wooden form shapes the shoveled, sifted, and wet earth. Every 4 to 5 inches, a metal tamper hits the soil until it rings as it would if it were hitting stone. The result is a house with 12- to 18-inch-thick walls that are resistant to fire and insects, practically soundproof, and have a high amount of thermal mass. When the sun hits the earthen walls, it takes so long for the heat to transmit that the house stays cool during the hottest part of the day. But the insulation value of earth is low, so in very cold climates, it may be necessary to add insulation to the outside. You may choose to cover the exterior with stucco and the interior with integral-color clay plaster or a clear sealant, or simply leave it uncovered. These walls are breathable and can sustain moisture penetration without damage as long as you don't cover the walls with anything that traps moisture. Cracks that form in the surface over time merely add to the beauty and character of the natural walls.

The French call this method of home building *pisé de terre*. California architect David Easton developed his own rammed-earth technique and named it PISE (pneumatically impacted stabilized earth). Rather than build a two-sided temporary form and shovel earth into it, he uses a pressure hose to spray the earth mixture onto a one-sided form. Metal reinforcement helps hold the wet material in place and adds strength. The earth is then screeded to a relatively smooth and even finish. This technique allows builders to construct rammed-earth homes more quickly.

Adobe

Homes made of adobe are similar in some ways to rammed-earth homes. The walls are made of a mixture of clay and sand, but the mix contains more water and is formed into bricks rather than built up with long horizontal forms level after level. Adobe bricks bake in the sun to harden, and then walls are constructed with mortar joints.

Adobe has high thermal mass but low insulating properties, so in colder climates, wrapping the adobe with insulation before applying siding is recommended. The exterior surface can be coated with mud plaster, lime plaster, stucco, or other breathable finishes. In some areas, adobe is left unfinished, but it must be protected by a roof with wide overhangs. Even when the material is protected, however, there can be structural or moisture problems if the home wasn't built well or site conditions such as groundwater levels have changed. Be sure that rainwater flows away from the building with the help of maintained gutter systems and proper soil grading.

ARCHITECT
PAULA BAKER-LAPORTE ON

Financing Unusual Construction Methods

New Mexico is one of the few places with an unbroken tradition of building with earth. We value these structures here. Adobe homes are worth more than their stick-built equals. Before committing to build this or any other type of earthen home, make sure you find a local bank that will lend you money, as sometimes financing can be hard to secure for non-traditional building techniques."

LEFT A curved cutout in an interior wall reminds visitors that this house is made of straw.

OPPOSITE PAGE, TOP LEFT White cedar shingles require little maintenance and give a house a pleasingly rustic look.

OPPOSITE PAGE, TOP RIGHT This straw-and-clay mixture creates a well-insulated home that stays cool and quiet inside.

OPPOSITE PAGE, BOTTOM Straw-and-clay homes have thick walls that allow for deep-set niches and windows.

Straw and Straw-Clay

In the late 1800s, Nebraska settlers began building houses out of straw—an agricultural waste product—because lumber for building was hard to come by. Since then, straw-bale houses have continued to be erected because the 14- to-24-inch-deep walls are strong, breathable, and well insulated, creating quiet and cool living spaces. Packing dry straw bales into the cavities of a post-and-beam framework is acceptable to most building inspectors, but you can also simply stack the packed straw without a frame so the straw itself holds up the roof. Without a wooden frame, the sizes of the structure and of openings for windows and doors are limited. Both sides of the straw-bale walls are then covered in chicken wire and coated with clay plaster to keep critters and moisture out. Drywall can also be used on interior walls.

Straw-bale homes are most common in dry climates because if moisture is allowed to seep into the walls, mold can grow and cause the straw to rot. If built and plastered

CONTRACTOR
JASON LEAR ON

Rain Screens

Stick-built homes constructed in areas with a lot of rainfall often use a rain-screen approach to siding. I build all of my houses this way in Seattle. The basic idea is to hold the siding off the drainage plane so that water can drain freely and everything stays dry. The exterior wall is covered with an impermeable drainage layer. Vents at the top and bottom of each wall promote airflow so that moisture doesn't get trapped behind the siding. The vents are then covered with bug screens."

correctly, however, a straw-bale house can do well in areas that are prone to rain and snow.

To reduce the risk of moisture damage, some builders mix the straw with clay to create a light clay/straw wall construction. Architect Paula Baker-Laporte considers this method the best of both worlds, as it continues to have great thermal mass, insulating, and soundproofing qualities.

Siding Options

When building a rammed-earth or adobe house, you may choose to leave the exterior walls unfinished. But every other method described in the previous pages requires some form of siding. Traditional choices include stucco, wood, fiber cement, and shingles. Architect Eric Corey Freed likes stucco because you can add color to the wet mix and avoid ever having to paint the house, making it a low-maintenance option. He also likes to use a fiber-cement siding product called SIL-LEED. "It comes in better colors than other brands, and we like to use it in board-and-batten patterns, alternating with natural wood to give it a modern, cool look," he says.

Architect Matt Elliott uses a lot of natural wood shingles because his clients like the low-maintenance benefits. "Red cedar shingles have more preservatives in them, so they last longer on a horizontal surface. But on vertical surfaces, they tend to turn black. White cedar shingles also last a long time on vertical surfaces and turn a silvery gray over time," he says. Even though cedar shingles repel water well, Elliott believes it's critical to have a rain-screen detail behind it (see box at left). "Older houses had boards with gaps under the shingles that allowed them to dry out, but we don't do that as often, because we're trying to build tighter houses. So now you need to build in a rain screen to avoid problems with rotting," he says.

The options for low- and no-VOC exterior paint are expanding. Choosing these products is better for the environment, but they are not as inherently durable outdoors as oil-based paint once many of the chemical ingredients are removed, so you will likely need to repaint sooner. Don't let this dissuade you from trying them, especially brands with proven outdoor track records. Also, when painting your siding, consider a light color for the majority of the surface. "Darker paint fades more quickly and absorbs more sunlight," says architect Peter Pfeiffer.

This flat-roofed adobe house catches rainwater to irrigate the surrounding landscape.

Homes built with energy efficiency in mind should include roofing material that is durable, low maintenance, and reflective. White or light-colored roofs reduce heat gain, keeping the overall temperature of the roof low so that heat isn't transferred into the house. Many eco-friendly homes have standing-seam metal roofs, which are low maintenance and light in color and also reflect the sun. Photovoltaic panels are easily clipped on, or film panels can be nestled between the seams. Metal is also good for collecting rainwater to reuse in the landscape. Other options include light-colored concrete, clay, or stone tiles; wood shakes; asphalt composition; or tar and gravel for flat roofs. Asphalt composition shingles are a popular choice because of their low price point and long life. If you select them, choose a light color that helps reflect the sun rather than the typical black or gray.

Flat roofs are common on adobe houses and those with a modern architectural style. When architect Eric Corey Freed builds a flat-roofed house, he uses polyiso (polyisocyanurate) foam as an insulator and finish material in one. Look for products by manufacturers that use pentane as the blowing agent rather than an ozone-depleting material.

ARCHITECT
PETER PFEIFFER ON THE

Energy Impact of Roofing

If you have a light-colored roof with a radiant barrier underneath, large overhangs, foam insulation, and low-e glass in your windows, you've made tremendous headway in the energy efficiency of your home for not much money. The right roof system with a radiant barrier can save you as much power as you'll get with a $50,000 solar system. Plus, it will add to the comfort quotient of your home and maybe even reduce your insurance premiums."

"You end up with a 2- to 6-inch-thick mass that, once hardened, creates a super-insulated, leak-proof roof. There are no seams, which is good from a maintenance standpoint," Freed says.

Ask your builder to include a radiant barrier in the attic. This material, which can come laminated to the back of OSB roof decking or attached on-site, blocks approximately 90 percent of a roof deck's radiant heat from entering the attic, making your living space much cooler. The radiant barrier works in conjunction with the air intakes and exhaust in the roof, allowing heat from the roof's surface to escape quickly so it isn't pushed down into the attic. "Also include a waterproofing membrane under the roofing material as an extra layer of insurance against leaks," advises architect Michelle Kaufmann.

TOP LEFT A light-colored asphalt composition roof reflects sunlight and should last around 20 years.

TOP RIGHT Metal roofs have many eco-friendly features and look great on modern-style homes.

BOTTOM Light wood shakes won't transfer heat from the sun into the house, and they are often the best choice for country- or Craftsman-style cottages.

Green Roofs

Native landscaping seamlessly extends onto the roof of this house built into the side of a hill.

Plants blossoming atop the roof of a home is still an unusual sight to behold. Beyond the attractive qualities of a house that blends in with its natural surroundings, a green roof has many environmental benefits.

To create a green roof, you can apply a waterproof membrane, lightweight soil, and low-maintenance plants, or you can assemble a modular green-roof system that clicks together and contains everything from roof protection to seedlings. Extensive green roofs, which feature low groundcovers and 2 to 4 inches of soil, are more common than intensive green roofs, which require several feet of soil and look more like a natural landscape with a variety of plant heights. The plant choices for green roofs depend on your climate and average rainfall, but in general they should be spreading plants that have a high drought tolerance. Sometimes an irrigation system is required, which adds to the weight of the roof and the cost of installation.

Up to 90 percent of a typical rainfall can be absorbed by a green roof, which reduces the drainage requirements of the surrounding building and the amount of rainwater that picks up pollutants on its way to storm drains. A water-retention layer sits on top of the waterproof membrane and under the plant, soil, and drainage layers of a green roof. Before installing a system, consult a builder or engineer to make sure your roof can handle the extra weight from heavy rainfall.

Green roofs will make the interior of the building more comfortable and will save you money on maintenance and energy costs. The waterproof membrane installed beneath the soil and plants protects the roof surface from ultraviolet rays and temperature fluctuation, thereby greatly increasing the life span of the roof and providing energy savings by keeping the house cooler. Green roofs also make the inside of the house quieter and lower the air temperature surrounding the house.

"Urban heat island" is a term that describes overheating in urban and suburban areas compared with rural areas because of the extensive paved and built surfaces that attract heat. Increased temperatures result in more air-conditioning and electricity usage, which is harmful to the environment. Cities like Chicago have paid close attention to this phenomenon and have

ARCHITECT
ERIC COREY FREED ON THE

Logistics of Green Roofs

I have two concerns about green roofs: the weight—which is about the same as water, about 62 pounds per cubic foot, assuming the worst after a heavy rain—and the drainage. It's not always possible to install on an existing roof because of these issues. Some old roofs just aren't strong enough. If you live in an area with a moist climate like Washington or Oregon, consider just planting moss on a shingle roof and letting it grow. I call it a poor man's version of a green roof."

implemented incentive programs for buildings that install green roofs in the city to counteract the effect.

Grid systems cost approximately $8 per square foot, or it can cost $12 to $24 per square foot to build a green roof from scratch. Although it increases the life span of the roof, the overall installation and material cost is about three times that of a standard roof, and the concept works best on flat roofs or those without much of a pitch. But the added cost can be worth it, especially if you can see and enjoy the green roof from upper-story windows.

TOP LEFT Grasses are a popular choice for green roofs. Note the sprinkler heads around the perimeter.

BOTTOM LEFT In a congested area of downtown Kansas City, one roof stands out. Residents of the building enjoy lush plantings among sitting areas, and there's even a section of the rooftop garden just for dogs.

TOP RIGHT Sometimes wildflower seeds will land surreptitiously on the roof and take hold, creating seasonal bursts of color.

BOTTOM RIGHT A modular system was used to create the green roof on this residential building in downtown Chicago. Annuals, perennials, and grasses ensure a mix of heights and seasonal interest, and the seating area in the center of the rooftop garden encourages residents to enjoy the view.

Solar Panels

Nothing screams "environmentally conscious home" quite like a swath of solar panels on the roof. While the cost of these systems can be prohibitive, more companies are offering solar lease programs, whereby you don't have to pay a high lump sum in advance, just monthly payments that might be equivalent to or lower than your current utility bill. With these new cost-effective options, more people than ever are signing up to have solar panels installed on their roofs. But solar energy is not a solution for every household.

If you live in a well-insulated home with a tight building envelope and have energy-efficient appliances, use CFL light bulbs, turn off lights when you aren't in a room, keep your thermostat turned down, turn off electrical equipment when it's not in use, and rarely if ever use an air conditioner, you most likely won't get any savings from solar panels. The only way that switching to a solar system would be cheaper than buying electricity from your local utility would be if you spend at least $120 to $150 a month right now. Even if this is the case, experts recommend adding insulation and more efficient windows and appliances before adding solar panels, as it makes no sense to feed energy generated from the panels into a house that wastes it.

However, if you live in a large and otherwise energy-efficient home but need to use your air-conditioning for many months out of the year,

or if you have more electric than gas-run appliances, installing solar panels is a smart decision. Some people who are marginal in this cost equation choose to swap gas-powered appliances for electric ones just to make the system worthwhile. It's possible to have your entire home run on solar panels in this case. Many areas offer tax credits and rebate programs that can reduce your upfront costs.

Beyond cost savings, harnessing and using your own energy rather than relying on conventional power plants means less coal is being burned to produce electricity, and that has wide-reaching environmental benefits. If you gather enough energy, you can even send electricity back to the utility company, getting a credit on future bills just by sitting in your home and letting it bask in the sunlight. But if you generate more energy than you use in an entire year, the utility company generally does not cut you a check, so it's not a moneymaking scheme, just a money-saving opportunity.

Red market umbrellas are more eye-catching than the solar panels on the shake roof of this adobe house.

CONTRACTOR
IRIS HARRELL ON

Considering Future Electricity Needs

Electricity will only get more expensive in the coming years. Hopefully, there will also be more electric cars on the road that will need to be powered, but we don't want that burden to go to conventional power plants that pollute our air. If you live in a sunny area, put as many solar panels on the roof as you can—not just a few to make you feel good. That way you're giving back to the utilities now and will be able to handle more electricity needs in the future."

LEFT These solar panels power the motor that heats the swimming pool below.

RIGHT A 4.5-kilowatt photovoltaic system covers the second-story roof of this Craftsman-style home.

Using Solar Panels in Cold Areas

We are finding that solar is an up-and-coming technology in the Northeast. We're using solar thermal to preheat water before taking it to the boiler, which cuts energy requirements considerably. More and more people have been incorporating solar panels in the past few years, despite the cold weather. On a cost basis, it's still marginal at best. But with energy prices going as they are, it will flip soon, so people understand that until solar energy reaches a critical mass, it will be expensive."

Installation Issues

When you call a solar company about installation, you will be asked many questions, including how much you generally spend on electricity. If you seem like a good candidate for solar, the company will do a site evaluation. Your roof needs to be strong enough to support the panels, and new enough that you won't have to dismantle the system to redo the roof anytime soon. Installers like to see south-facing roofs without surrounding large trees, but any direction other than north can still work well enough to be worth it. The panels need to get a minimum of four hours of direct sunlight per day. It's possible to install the panels on a garage, on an arbor, or even on the ground if your home's roof isn't appropriate.

Be sure you buy or lease a solar energy system from a reputable dealer that uses proven, high-quality equipment. A good solar company will also monitor the performance of the system, supply you with data, perform any maintenance needed, and offer a warranty on parts and installation.

Hardscaping

Composite decking is a great choice for an outdoor room like this because you don't have to worry about getting splinters in bare feet.

Patios, decks, and paths define activity areas in your front and back yards and lead you from one destination to the next. The materials you choose will influence the style and function of your outdoor living spaces and will indicate whether your garden is meant to be traveled through efficiently or leisurely. And as elsewhere in the house, there are plenty of sustainable, healthful material options.

Think about creating outdoor rooms with your hardscaping choices. These are areas built for specific activities, such as eating, playing, or simply lounging, and they will make your overall home feel more spacious.

Decking

When a site is sloped or uneven, adding a deck makes more sense than excavating for a patio. Decks can be transitions from one space to the next, or destinations of their own. While the size of a deck depends upon how much of the yard you want to turn over for this purpose, the shape and the way it connects to the landscape beyond have more to do with the style of your garden and of the house. Surround the deck with nature by working curves or uneven edges into the landscape in an organic way. For a large deck, allow nature through in the form of cutouts for existing trees, ring the perimeter with

ABOVE A small wooden deck in the middle of the garden, surrounded by tropical plants and covered with sheer fabric, is a restful place to sit and read on a lazy summer day.

LEFT Cutouts that allow trees or grasses to grow within the deck will help tie the structure in with the rest of the backyard.

RIGHT Untreated decking will turn a weathered gray, which looks great surrounding this modern-style farmhouse.

plants, and add pots of flowers or bamboo that help direct foot traffic.

If you're building a wooden deck, choose wood that was grown locally or that is certified by the Forest Stewardship Council (FSC). Pressure-treated wood lasts longer outdoors than untreated wood, but many materials used to treat wood are not environmentally friendly. Look for wood treated with ammoniacal copper quaternary (ACQ) or copper azole (CA), in which copper is the active ingredient that will prevent the boards from rotting. There is also composite decking, made of recycled plastic and sawdust. High-quality composites mimic the grain pattern of natural wood, don't splinter, and don't need regular sanding and resealing like wood does. Composites are often a more sustainable choice because they are made of recycled materials and are virtually maintenance-free. Another option is locally grown redwood, which naturally resists insects and decay without chemical treatments and doesn't need much maintenance if you don't mind it graying over time.

ARCHITECT
MICHELLE KAUFMANN ON

Seamless Transitions

In the homes I design, my goal is to blur the boundary between interior and exterior spaces. I love using accordion-style glass doors that can be pushed off to the side when open. I also try to extend interior flooring materials to an adjoining deck or patio when possible so that the transition from inside to outside is seamless. For stone flooring, we use grout in the joints inside the house and transition to gravel outdoors so that water can move through the gaps, making it a permeable surface."

Patios

LEFT Instead of a solid concrete patio, these concrete tiles are spaced slightly apart and are surrounded by low-lying ground-cover so that water can percolate into the soil.

RIGHT A casual, decomposed granite patio is inexpensive, blends into the landscape, and does not cause drainage problems.

A patio just outside the back door serves as a transition between indoor and outdoor spaces, bridging the gap between the protection of the house and the openness of the yard. Patios can also be built in the center or at the edges of the backyard—as destination points or to carve out an area for a particular activity, such as dining or lounging by the pool.

Before deciding on patio materials, consider the style and proportions of the house. Study the house for patterns and details you can mimic on the patio, and look to the window and door dimensions to guide your decisions on scale. Your landscape architect or builder will make sure the patio is

graded away from the house so you won't have a problem with standing water, or water traveling into the home. Soften the edges of the patio with plants to provide a natural transition between hardscape and landscape.

Stone patios have an elegant look. To minimize carbon emissions, choose stone that was quarried within 300 miles of your house. Local stone will also look more natural in the landscape, especially when paired with native plants. Brick patios work with many home styles. Before buying new materials, check local salvage yards for bricks that may have come from a nearby property. Recycled bricks have more character but can sometimes cost more

than new bricks. Be sure to lay stone and bricks on sand rather than concrete and with enough space between each piece to allow rainwater to seep into the ground. Otherwise, rainwater that flows from the solid surface directly into storm drains can pick up chemicals and toxins on its journey, contaminating natural waterways.

Because traditional concrete patios are not permeable, the only way to make them more eco-friendly used to be to incorporate fly ash into the mix—a byproduct of the coal industry that would otherwise end up in landfills—and to use soy-based or otherwise nontoxic stains and sealants. But now a special kind of concrete is available

that does allow rainwater to seep through the material into the ground. Permeable concrete is made without a sand binder and with little water and a higher amount of cement and fly ash than standard concrete mixes. The result is a bubbly-looking, rough surface. But even when compacted with debris, the material allows water to percolate through at a rate of 3 inches per hour, virtually eliminating runoff. This is a bigger deal for the environment in a 5,000-square-foot parking lot than on a 300-square-foot patio, but if you're pouring a new concrete slab, it's worth considering. You can also find permeable concrete pavers.

LEFT Antique brick set in sand provides a stable surface for a vintage iron table and chairs.

RIGHT The rough surface of local flagstone is softened by creeping woolly thyme.

ABOVE An arbor constructed with thick wooden columns and beams provides shade for a flagstone patio.

LEFT This vintage iron headboard painted gold and lilac supports a creeping vine.

OPPOSITE PAGE When the wisteria vine grows in, it will help keep this side of the house cooler in summer.

Trellises and Arbors

A trellis is a small structure often covered in vines or flowers that adds height and dimension to a garden. Use recycled wood, metal, or a reclaimed item such as an old coat rack to ornament the garden and hold up climbing plants and vegetables. An arbor is a larger structure that can provide shade, direct foot traffic, and establish an architectural sense of permanence in the yard. Again, this is a great opportunity to use recycled materials, such as wood from trees that had to be removed from your property or stone left over from another project. If you use new wood, choose something that is locally grown or is FSC-certified. Finish it with a low- or no-VOC paint or stain and sealant.

Study the sun patterns on your property before committing to the location and size of your arbor. Design the structure to provide relief from the summer sun but allow winter sun to make its way into the house. One way to do this is to grow a plant over the top of the arbor that will be in full bloom during the summer, providing shade, but that dies back in the winter.

Play Areas

Active children can quickly take over a backyard, and a parent's goal is to create a fun but safe space to play. Some families will decide to incorporate a play structure such as a treehouse, or equipment that encourages sporting activities. Others may forgo play equipment in favor of a garden that inspires imagination with kid-friendly plants and structures that can be turned into a pirate ship one day and a castle the next. Whichever direction you choose, try to create spaces that encourage multiple activities and that will grow and change as your kids do.

Structures such as playhouses and treehouses are a great way to use recycled materials in the garden. Search online and at local salvage yards for old lumber, discarded doors, single-pane windows, and even hardwood flooring and plumbing fixtures. Be sure the indoor air quality will be healthful by using no- or low-VOC paints, stains, and sealants.

Sandboxes are a treat for young kids, but there are several health issues to consider. Choose a spot in the garden that gets a few hours of sun during the day to keep the sand dry and sanitary. Keep animals from using the sandbox by incorporating a fitted hard top or a mesh cover. And stay away from "play sand" that may contain fine shards of crystalline silica, which has been linked to lung disease in people who are exposed to it daily.

Areas that will be used for climbing, riding, or jumping should have surrounding surfaces that are safe to land on. Grass is commonly used for this purpose, but it doesn't provide much padding for falls and it's not an eco-friendly choice because of the amount of water and maintenance it requires. Sand and pea gravel are easily tracked around the garden; become compacted from rain, making the surface much harder; and are favorite spots for pets and other animals. Recycled-wood chips provide better cushioning for falls but must be leveled and replaced fairly often. The best material in areas where kids may fall off high swings or climbing structures is rubber mulch. It's not appealing to animals, does not deteriorate or become compacted, and is available in many colors. Look for recycled rubber—but not tire rubber, as it can offgas.

TOP LEFT This eco-friendly playhouse features a green roof, recycled leaded-glass windows, and a reclaimed panel door. When it's no longer needed as a play structure, it will make a great potting shed.

TOP MIDDLE When not in use, sandboxes should be covered to protect it from pets and other animals visiting your yard.

TOP RIGHT Wood chips make a suitable landing surface for swings as long as swings don't fly too high into the air.

BOTTOM LEFT Look in building salvage yards to find used or overstock windows for playhouses and treehouses.

BOTTOM RIGHT A clever reuse of old cardboard boxes makes a perfect refuge.

One of the best ways to make your home more eco-friendly is to reduce water use. By now, you hopefully have plans to switch out your old water-guzzling toilets, faucets, and appliances and are ready to look to the rest of your property for more savings. Your goal should be a landscape that incorporates as many native plants as possible that require little to no irrigation. But there are lots of little changes you can make if you aren't ready to rip out your entire yard.

Also consider that what you do outside will have an effect inside. Work with a landscape professional to plan for trees that will shade your house in summer and allow sunlight through in winter. A mature landscape with well-placed trees and shrubs can make a big difference in the amount of heat or air-conditioning you need.

Plant Natives

Xeriscaping is a landscape principle that aims to reduce water use by combining native plants, permeable hard-scaping, and smaller lawns. The idea is to create a garden that works with nature rather than against it. Along those lines, keeping up a lush lawn in a desert doesn't make as much sense as planting succulents and cactus that have grown and thrived in that environment for centuries. Likewise, a rainy climate can sustain grass, particularly some ornamental varieties, with little intervention. If you are able to start from scratch, select native, water-conserving plants and group them by water need.

Practice organic gardening by not using chemical fertilizers or toxic pest killers. Soil that is aerated and fed with organic compost shouldn't need much fertilizer, but if your plants do require an extra boost, feed them with a store-bought organic product. Another natural solution is to create habitats for beneficial insects and animals that will police your yard for pests that might damage it.

This native garden bursting with lavender and ornamental grasses requires minimal water.

The types of plants that grow naturally in your area will be low-maintenance, hardy choices for your landscape.

TOP Solar-powered lanterns can be hung in trees throughout the garden to create a festive mood without using any electricity from your local utility.

BOTTOM LEFT Composted leaves were turned into mulch and spread around newly planted shrubs and groundcovers.

BOTTOM RIGHT Gathered pine needles can be put to good use as mulch material.

OPPOSITE PAGE A minimal amount of low-voltage or solar-powered lighting will allow you to enjoy the landscape after dark without creating light pollution.

you won't waste water by irrigating an area where only half of the plants need it regularly. Drip-irrigation systems reduce water runoff and put the water right where it's needed, at the roots of plants, as opposed to sprinkler systems that often overshoot their targets or produce a spray that gets carried away by the wind. Whatever system you choose, incorporate weather sensors that will react to heat by watering more often and respond to rain by shutting off.

Landscape lighting is an important safety element, but don't overdo it and contribute to light pollution. Place lights carefully to guide people along pathways and illuminate steps and borders. There are many attractive designs for landscape lighting powered by low voltage or photovoltaics.

Reduce Waste

Instead of letting the garbage collector haul off tons of your landscape debris each year, start composting your plant waste to feed back into the soil, and save excess topsoil for future landscape projects (or give it to someone who can use it). You can also create your own mulch using pruned branches. All of your plants should have a 2- to 3-inch layer of mulch around them to keep the ground moist, which in turn will reduce the amount of irrigation they need. Avoid store-bought mulch that comes from forests. If you can't create your own mulch, buy local and organic varieties that are made with recycled content.

Irrigation and Lighting

Once your plants are grouped by water need, plan a high-efficiency irrigation system that waters each section as much or as little as necessary. That way,

ARCHITECT
MATT ELLIOTT ON

Native Landscapes

We work with our clients to create native landscapes that require a minimum amount of irrigation and maintenance. Here in Maine, plants like blueberries and ferns will thrive with no interference. In general, our clients aren't looking for big lawns."

Rainwater Collection

Saving rainwater to irrigate your landscape is a responsible and proactive response to the water shortages that many areas now face. But there are still some states that actually consider rainwater state property and do not allow people to catch or reuse it. These laws are slowly changing, but before investing in a rainwater catchment system, call your local building department to make sure it's legal in your area.

Systems range from simple and almost decorative setups to massive tanks buried in your backyard. If you have a small patio with few plants to water, replace one or two of your gutter downspouts with a rain chain that guides rainwater into a small rock-covered basin buried underground. The water can then be pumped out and used to irrigate potted plants and borders.

The next step up is using larger containers such as rain barrels, which typically hold about 60 gallons. Barrels set up for this purpose have an intake valve that hooks up to your gutter downspout and passes rainwater into the barrel. A

spigot at the bottom of the barrel allows you to fill a watering can. Many barrels come with a screen to keep leaves out of the water while you have the solid cover removed to allow the water to breathe after each new rainfall.

However, to really make a large dent in your irrigation water use, you need to invest in a cistern or tank. Aboveground tanks can range in capacity from a couple of hundred to a couple of thousand gallons, or you can bury a 10,000-gallon tank in the yard during a major landscape project. This can also be a great way to fill in an old swimming pool that is no longer wanted. Pipes leading from the roof and gutter system snake over to buried cisterns from every side of the house, and irrigation pipes pump the water out into sprinkler and drip heads.

"Many of my clients ask why they should collect water for the yard at all," says architect Eric Corey Freed. "Why not use xeriscape principles to reduce our water needs instead? Often the most practical solution is a combination of the two: water collection and landscape water-use reduction."

OPPOSITE PAGE, LEFT Rainwater flows in dramatic fashion from wide-mouthed gutters into a dry creek surrounding the garden. The water is then filtered into an underground cistern and reused.

OPPOSITE PAGE, RIGHT Plastic barrels fit nicely at the base of a raised patio, placed under each gutter downspout. They collect enough water to irrigate potted plants around the garden.

ABOVE A rain chain guides water into this burlap-wrapped container.

RIGHT This copper pipe leads from the roof to an underground cistern that feeds the drip-irrigation system for the entire yard.

In New Mexico, new homes larger than 2,500 square feet are required to collect rainwater for irrigation. "Most often, when you look at the whole budget, it makes sense to collect rainwater for the garden and gray water [see pages 98–99] for larger orchards where the soil needs to be recharged," says architect Paula Baker-Laporte.

ARCHITECT
PETER PFEIFFER ON

Maintaining Rainwater-Collection Systems

Rainwater collection is an active water-conservation system, as opposed to a passive water-conservation system, such as using native plants or installing ultra high-efficiency toilets. You have to be an engaged homeowner to get something out of a rainwater-collection system over the years. There will be a constant need for clearing out gutters, checking filters, and cleaning out sprinkler heads. I have a 3,000-gallon tank in my backyard, but that's really not enough storage to help the city's water supply when it's not raining. I think that unless you invest in a much larger system, you'll do just as much good having a landscape that is truly drought-tolerant in your climate once the plants have matured."

Reducing Lawns

The traditional American landscape has seemingly always included an expanse of lush, green grass. People took great pride in the condition of their lawns and spent large amounts of time each weekend fertilizing and mowing them.

Today, the watering requirements of a sizable lawn are not only financially out of reach in some areas but downright wasteful, given the water shortages across the globe. Plus, the gas-powered mowers that maintain lawns spew emissions that pollute our air. But it doesn't have to be all or nothing.

If you love the look and functionality of grass, keep a small area of it and choose a variety that can survive on little water and needs less fertilizer.

Make sure the type you select will grow in the amount of sun or shade your yard gets throughout the day. If you live in a desert climate, though, any amount of lawn will require a lot of water, so it makes more sense to eliminate grass altogether.

Depending on your climate, you may get more bang for your buck with a meadow of ornamental grass rather than a traditional lawn. Requiring no more than four mowings per year, ornamental grasses create a lush, undulating area perfect for playing. Many varieties require little supplemental water. Be sure you select the right ones for your area, as some can be invasive and others won't survive a frost.

Another option that makes sense in hot climates or in yards with too much shade to grow a lawn is synthetic grass. You can now find products that mimic natural varieties of grass, such as Kentucky blue, fescue, and rye. For a price, it's possible to get the look you want with no watering or mowing, and it stands up to kids and pets as well. Choose a synthetic lawn that is made with recycled materials.

To remove part or all of your current lawn, avoid spraying it with chemicals to kill the roots or digging it up and sending it to the landfill. Instead, use a technique called sheet mulching. Place several layers of recycled cardboard over the lawn so that sunlight can't reach it. Then cover the cardboard with topsoil and mulch. Plant native, low-water plants in the area right away, and over time the grass will die and the cardboard will decompose into the soil below.

OPPOSITE PAGE In this front yard, the lawn was greatly reduced with the addition of a retaining wall made of recycled concrete. Ornamental grasses and shrubs below need little supplemental water.

TOP LEFT Instead of planting traditional grass that can be hard to maintain around steppingstones, grow a variety of ornamental grasses that need only infrequent mowing and create a graceful softness in the garden.

TOP RIGHT Spreading groundcovers can be a functional replacement for grass and don't need as much water.

BOTTOM SYNLawn looks like natural grass, saves water, and stays green in shady areas.

Kitchen Gardens

People who desire to live a more organic and eco-friendly lifestyle often decide to grow some of their own fruits and vegetables after years of shopping at their local farmers' markets. Not only is it a great way to be able to eat organic food for less, but it also teaches children where food comes from and fills them with a sense of pride when they've helped create their own meals.

If you've had little to no gardening experience, it's a good idea to start small with one or two raised beds. It's easier to manage a kitchen garden in raised beds than in the ground. Most exist-

ing soil needs a lot of amending to grow organic food. Plus it's not comfortable working on your knees: with raised beds, you can build in ledges for sitting on. But don't make the beds wider than 3 or 4 feet or you'll have trouble reaching the center. No room for a raised bed? Try mixing edibles such as herbs and lettuces with your border plants or growing them in pots.

Placement

The first step in creating a kitchen garden is deciding what you want to grow. Research what grows best in your climate,

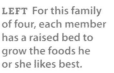

LEFT For this family of four, each member has a raised bed to grow the foods he or she likes best.

TOP This is what it's all about: organic carrots pulled from the family garden.

BOTTOM No room for a raised bed? Try growing herbs or lettuces in pots.

check the sun and water requirements for each variety, and then group plants with similar needs. It's not always possible to plant edibles near the kitchen, but you can always take advantage of the need to pick a few tomatoes for dinner as an excuse to meander through the garden. Find the best spot for what you want to grow and let the size of the area determine how many raised beds you can have. With careful planning, you'll be able to enjoy the fruits of your labor in every season.

Outdoor Furniture

This rusted iron table-and-chair set still has beauty and serves a purpose. The chairs are made more comfortable with cushions, which are moved indoors when not in use.

Just like indoor furnishings, the furniture you select for your yard should be built to last and made of eco-friendly or recycled materials. Avoid the temptation to buy inexpensive outdoor furniture. You may reason that it's going to be outside and that it's therefore pointless to pay for quality when the furniture might get ruined anyway. In fact, buying inexpensive furniture will ensure that outcome. Low-quality materials and finishes won't stand up to the elements, and the pieces will soon end up in a landfill. You will save money in the long run if you buy well-made pieces that will last, and it's the more eco-friendly choice as well.

Materials and Finishes

Look for furniture made of wood harvested from sustainably managed forests and constructed with mortise-and-tenon joinery. Marine-quality hardware and finishes will go a long way toward ensuring that pieces won't rust or be damaged by water. While wicker furniture seems outdoorsy, it won't last long outside. Wicker look-alikes made of a weatherproof resin will resist fading, cracking, and tearing, but they are made of plastic and will not biodegrade. Metal furniture looks great outdoors; look for something made of recycled metal and keep it sealed so it won't rust over time.

Vintage and flea-market furniture is a great option for outdoors, as it adds style for less money. Even if a piece doesn't last forever, at least you are able to get some more use out of something that would have otherwise gone to waste.

ABOVE Dress up a worn table with a vintage tablecloth or quilt for outdoor lunches.

RIGHT A wooden picnic table and painted tin cups and plates are functional choices that will withstand the elements.

BELOW Invest in high-quality furniture that turns your outdoor living space into somewhere you want to spend time.

INTERIOR DESIGNER
KELLY LAPLANTE ON

Outdoor Fabric

At this time, there are no eco-friendly fabrics that will last outdoors, but I'm hoping that someone comes up with a solution soon. Fabrics currently on the market that are meant to be left outdoors are treated with toxic chemicals, so you want to avoid those. For now, I use remnant fabrics for outdoors, so at least it's not something that's new production that will end up in a landfill after a few seasons."

ABOVE An industrial-size metal tub is now used as a container for bamboo, which should not be planted straight into the ground, as it is invasive. The garden gate puts an old glass front door to good use.

LEFT A piece of architectural salvage nestled among the rocks appears as though it has always been in the garden.

RIGHT Pots of varying heights look almost like pins at the end of a bowling alley, while the two black ceramic balls lie in wait for a strike.

Garden Art

There are many eco-friendly materials that can be used to dress up your garden. Recycled objects are the most fun and can add unique style to the landscape. Large objects that would overwhelm an indoor space are a better match for the height and grandeur of the outdoors. Search for objects that inspire you, and snap them up even if they aren't usually seen in a garden. Almost any container can serve as a planter if you drill a couple of holes in the bottom. Old wine barrels and metal sinks are often reused in this way. You can also use pots and pans and even old shoes.

Architectural salvage, such as shutters or stone pillars, can lend a sense of permanence to a grouping of plants. Old single-pane windows that weren't energy efficient in their original purpose can be hung from the edge of a patio roof to frame a particularly lovely view of the garden. Once you start hunting around, you'll see why incorporating recycled materials as outdoor art has become so popular.

Chapter 7

Getting It Done

Now that we've been through each part of the house and garden and discussed eco-friendly changes you can make, it's time to think about executing your plan. Whether you will embark on a small remodeling project or a major renovation, or plan to build a new green home, you will likely need to rely on the help of professionals like the ones we've been hearing from throughout the book. This chapter explains who can do what and walks you through the process of finding the best people. It also discusses the costs of building green; getting rid of construction waste responsibly; and keeping your indoor air quality healthful during a remodel.

Creating Your Green Home

This well-utilized space built with eco-friendly materials gets plenty of natural light, and the concrete floor is kept warm with hydronic radiant heating.

There are many ways to create a healthier home, from avoiding materials that will offgas toxins to using eco-friendly cleaning products. And there are many ways to make your home more energy and water efficient, such as adding insulation, fixing leaky windows, using compact fluorescent lightbulbs, replacing water-guzzling appliances, landscaping with drought-resistant plants, and possibly adding solar panels to your roof. Try not to get overwhelmed with your to-do list if you live in a home that needs a lot of improving to be considered green. There's no point in looking backward; just resolve to make your home as eco-friendly and healthful as possible from today onward. Little by little, the eco-friendly materials and furnishings you buy and the improvements you undertake over time will make a difference.

Hiring Green Professionals

Every year more and more people are getting green certifications and making the products and services they offer more environmentally responsible. So it won't be difficult to find people who claim they can make your home greener. But ask some questions to make sure they really do know their stuff. Look for a personal understanding of and commitment to the issues through the stories they tell and the past work they show. After reading this book, you will be able to tell those who are truly informed from those who just want you to think they are. Depending on the scope of your project, the professionals described on the following pages may be of service to you.

ABOVE The walls of this cabin were constructed with structural insulated panels (see page 148). Metal roofing and siding deflect sunlight, reducing the need for air-conditioning.

RIGHT Low louvered windows draw cool air and breezes into the house.

BELOW Buying reclaimed-wood furniture and bringing potted plants indoors are two easy ways to start living green.

ARCHITECT
MATT ELLIOTT ON

Setting Priorities

Green building is such a wide-ranging topic. Most often we can't accomplish everything in one home, so we ask our clients what's most important to them. Is it your own health, the condition of the planet, the health of the workers who make these materials? Most people are concerned about all of these things, but if you can pick the ones that are most important to you, the project can have that focus. If you build it well, insulate it well, and put in a good heating system, you're halfway there. Take one step at a time, focusing first on the structure and then on the finish materials. Otherwise, you'll get overwhelmed about how many concerning issues there are."

ARCHITECTS are state-licensed professionals who can help you with a major remodel or addition, or design a new house. They are the ones to rely on for design work that involves structural issues. For a remodel, they will make sure that the plans work with the style of the existing house and that your existing mechanical systems can handle the proposed changes. Architects can produce the building plans needed for permits, help you choose materials, negotiate bids from contractors, and in some cases supervise the project.

GENERAL CONTRACTORS usually specialize in construction, but some have design skills as well.

Depending on the size of the company you hire, a general contractor may do all the work alone or hire subcontractors for specific parts of the job. Contractors can order supplies and materials for you, if that's part of your arrangement, secure building permits, and schedule city inspections. If you want to end up with an eco-friendly home, look for general contractors who first and foremost build high-quality houses. Only these true craftsmen will take the time to construct something using techniques that create an energy-efficient space.

INTERIOR DESIGNERS are experts in color, texture, and style. They can help you with everything from

creating a color scheme to selecting furniture, fixtures, and accessories, such as window treatments and hardware. Some designers can manage the building aspects of your job, hiring subcontractors and keeping everything on schedule, while others will sketch the design and select products but leave the installation phase to someone else.

While many designers are members of the American Society of Interior Designers (ASID), interior designer Kelly LaPlante believes it's more important to ask whether a designer is LEED-certified (see page 25). "You want to make sure your designer is aware of all the issues so they don't select a no-VOC paint but then purchase conventional furniture," she says.

LANDSCAPE DESIGNERS can advise you on which plants will thrive in your garden with little supplemental water. Most landscape designers are willing to work on small projects and charge by the hour. What you spend on their advice will most likely save you from wasting money on plants that wouldn't survive in your yard. If you are creating an entirely new landscape that involves challenging site issues, or if you need retaining walls, have drainage problems, or must apply for a permit, you may require the services of a landscape architect. In either case, select someone who specializes in native plants and low-water landscapes.

LEFT Interior designers find furniture, window treatments, rugs, and accessories that combine to create a certain feel. Untreated fabrics keep the air quality in this room healthful.

RIGHT This landscape filled with succulents looks lush and requires very little water.

DESIGN-BUILD FIRMS are companies that have project managers, architects, contractors, and interior designers all on staff. They can be worth the price for large projects, especially when you don't have time to be involved daily. For example, if you hire an architect to come up with a plan for a new home, that person might not be able to design something that will definitely meet your budget, because he or she may not build homes every day and therefore isn't as familiar with how much things cost. In a design-build firm, because contractors and project managers work with the architects from the start, it's more likely that the plan will meet your budget and schedule.

Contractor Iris Harrell owns a design-build firm and believes in the benefit of having the entire team on board from the start. "Say you have an architect design the house of your dreams, then you start bidding out the work and everything comes back too high. Many times this is the case, and the architect has to get paid for his or

LEFT This LEED Platinum home features a screened-in porch on one end of the first floor and a stair tower on the opposite side, providing passive thermal siphoning for natural cooling and ventilation.

RIGHT Healthful homes have plenty of fresh air and natural daylight and are free of clutter and synthetic materials.

her work but the house never gets built. That's a hard thing to go through. With a design-build firm, this scenario doesn't happen," Harrell says. There are also benefits when one project manager is in charge of a team that he or she has worked with before, rather than the homeowner having to deal directly with each professional and settle

miscommunications and resolve scheduling issues that come up between them. Finally, there's the benefit of time. "We can build a 2,300-square-foot house—design and construction—in one year," Harrell says. "Normally it would take a year to design the house and get the permits, and another year to build." If a design-build firm makes sense for the scope of your project, look for one with highly talented designers and builders who hold green certifications.

PROFESSIONAL ORGANIZERS can help you prepare for a remodeling project. In a kitchen, for example, an organizer will help you decide which tools, cookware, and dishes you really need. Then you can design your new kitchen knowing exactly how much storage is necessary. Even if you aren't remodeling, an organizer can declutter a space, making it easier to keep clean and therefore healthier. He or she will think of ways

to organize what you end up keeping so that things won't get out of place again. Be sure to hire someone who will take unwanted things to a charitable organization or help you recycle or sell them. The goal should be to throw as little as possible into the trash.

BAU-BIOLOGISTS are certified professionals who promote the use of healthful building practices to improve living and working spaces and the health of people who occupy them. They can be environmental inspectors and consultants, but there are also builders, architects, and medical practitioners who are particularly interested in how built spaces affect human health and so have made that a specialty. People who suffer from chemical sensitivity will benefit from the knowledge of bau-biologists who have tested materials for this purpose and can guide homeowners toward products that are less aromatic and contain zero VOCs.

Interviewing

You may have the greenest of intentions when embarking on a remodel, but if you hire someone who does not share your concerns for things like indoor air quality and reducing waste, your plans may not come to fruition. Therefore, hiring professionals for an eco-friendly project can be even more complicated, because you have to assess people's knowledge of and commitment to green building. There are some credentials you can look for (see pages 24–25), but even if those seem to be in order, it's important to check out people's past work for yourself by speaking to former clients to find out whether the pros practice what they preach.

To locate eco-friendly builders, architects, and designers, contact local green building organizations, as some keep lists of accredited professionals. You can also contact manufacturers and suppliers of green building materials for recommendations. If you have a friend or neighbor who recently embarked on an eco-friendly remodel, personal recommendations are best. Often if you can find one designer or builder who shares your goals for the house, he or she will lead you to others. In the end, you will probably have a mix of people working on the project: some with strong green credentials and beliefs and those who are new to the concept but eager to comply. Architect Matt Elliott suggests getting any subcontractors on board as early in the process as possible. "Tell them about your concerns and make them a part of the team rather than imposing your views on them. Talk about how they can help you make the project unfold the way you want it to," Elliott advises.

TOP LEFT Green builders and designers can help you find the best eco-friendly materials, like this IceStone countertop.

TOP RIGHT No electric lights are needed during the day in this second-story bedroom designed by architect Peter Pfeiffer. The space is kept cool with plenty of insulation, windows that allow for cross-ventilation, and a ceiling fan.

BOTTOM LEFT Large sliding glass doors provide a breathtaking view from the living room and allow prevailing winds and sunlight to enter the space. This is not by accident but by design.

BOTTOM RIGHT Architects designing with reuse in mind will find creative ways to integrate reclaimed materials. This bathroom vanity is made of local reclaimed wood.

Permits

When you're embarking on cosmetic projects such as painting, installing new flooring, or replacing an old plumbing fixture, you generally do not need a building permit. But if you are remodeling a bathroom or kitchen, adding on to your home, or putting in a new heating system, you will probably need to apply for a permit and go through the inspection process. Once you determine the scope of your job, take a sketch of the plans to your local building department to find out whether you need a permit and what the cost will be.

Sometimes people try to avoid the permit process because the fees can be high, the home's property taxes might increase, and waiting for inspectors to show up can complicate a schedule. But doing some types of construction work without a permit is illegal. If you get caught, you may be required to rip out the work and start from scratch. Your homeowner's insurance may be invalidated, and when you eventually sell the house, you may not be able to include the value of your improvements if you can't show that the work was permitted.

The building code is there for your safety and the safety of other people, including those working on your house.

Local inspectors will make sure the work is done correctly and to code, which protects you from shoddy work you might not have the expertise to detect.

However, there are some complications in getting building permits for certain types of green building. Architect Matt Elliott reports having some difficulty in his area when the building officials are slow to move out of their comfort zones. And in many places, the building code is out of date, so certain construction practices that might make perfect sense for energy efficiency aren't allowed, simply because the code hasn't caught up to newer and better ideas.

Don't let this discourage you. Go to the building department early in the process, explain what you want to do, and keep asking to talk to the next person up the ladder. Chances are that if the building technique is sound and what you're doing won't harm you or your neighbors, you will be allowed to do it.

TOP Sometimes the simplest solutions are the most eco-friendly. This pantry is situated on an exterior wall that has screened louvers to let in cool outdoor air. No electricity is used, but staples like nuts, grains, and potatoes are kept below room temperature.

MIDDLE A sunroom addition constructed with recycled materials will enlarge your living space but should not cause difficulties with the local building department.

BOTTOM There are many ways to save water in a bathroom, but low-flow showerheads, faucets, and toilets are the only ones that will pass most local inspections. Using gray water for toilets and diverting shower water to the landscape are currently not allowed in many places.

OPPOSITE PAGE Landscapes with swimming pools and steep grades require building permits, but using recycled concrete for the stairs will not pose a problem.

ARCHITECT
ERIC COREY FREED ON

Dealing with Local Planning Offices

You don't need to hire an architect who is best friends with everyone at your city's planning department office. It's better to get an architect who is extremely knowledgeable about eco-friendly systems so he or she can argue the issue effectively. The only challenges I come up against are with straw-bale construction and gray-water systems, but I never have any issue with eco-friendly finishing materials."

What Will It Cost?

A high-end custom kitchen like this is expensive any way you slice it, but building with energy and water efficiency in mind and using FSC-certified wood and no-VOC finishes will not blow the budget. You'll actually save money on your utility bills and create a healthier home in the long run.

The most repeated phrase of people who don't want to change their ways or haven't done their homework is "Green building is too expensive." While it was once true that green building materials were scarce enough to carry a premium, those days are behind us. Any well-informed and well-connected builder will tell you that building an energy-efficient and healthful home doesn't have to cost more than building a toxic home that wastes water and heat. Materials like FSC-certified wood, no-VOC paint, and formaldehyde-free insulation are now widely available. Depending on the product,

you'll pay the same price for comparable traditional building materials, or perhaps 5 percent more. But your reward will be far-reaching in that you will have built a home you will be able to afford 20 years from now, when prices for electricity, gas, and water have skyrocketed.

Beyond the cost of owning and operating a home is the cost of living in a house full of toxic materials. Architect Paula Baker-Laporte is often asked how much it costs to build a healthy green home. Her response: "Have you ever calculated how much it costs to be sick?" She once lived in a house full of formaldehyde-emitting materials that resulted in a long-term illness. "I calculated that my three-year stay in that house cost me $65 per square foot in medical bills."

Good health and quality of life are priceless. When you build or remodel a house, you make thousands of decisions. Make the ones that will benefit your well-being, including the size of your house, the amount of natural light you have, and the finish materials you surround yourself with.

There are, of course, some beautiful eco-friendly products, such as tiles or countertops made of recycled materials, that can cost a fair amount more than standard choices. Many companies that make things out of recycled materials are small businesses that don't enjoy the economies of scale their competitors do. A good number of them have also chosen to manufacture their products in the United States to keep jobs here and keep down their carbon footprint. If you come across an eco-friendly company whose business philosophy is in sync with your environmental values, support that business by paying a little more for its product. It may be true that you can buy a slab of imported granite for less money, but environmental and labor practices in many parts of the world are lax, so you may be supporting a manufacturer that is able to sell you a less expensive product by taking advantage of these circumstances. The more we support local businesses that recycle materials, use healthful ingredients, and pay living wages to people in your community, the sooner we will see their prices come down.

ARCHITECT
PETER PFEIFFER ON

Saving Money

My own house, in Austin, Texas, is a five-star green home (similar to LEED Gold certification). It is 4,100 square feet, and my average utility bill is $189 per month for gas and electricity. My neighbor has the same square footage, and he pays between $750 and $1,000 per month. Plus we have a swimming pool and he doesn't. My house is proof that a carefully designed, well-constructed, and tightly built structure that takes advantage of sun and wind patterns will save significant sums of money."

TOP Someone else's unwanted items can become featured treasures in your house and save you money. The cost of a built-in cabinet with this kind of storage space would have far exceeded the price of these old school lockers.

BOTTOM LEFT Instead of buying a wall shelf made of particleboard, choose recycled materials such as metal tubs hung on their sides and vintage hardware for hats and coats.

BOTTOM RIGHT Cabinets made of wheatboard and finished with no-VOC paint don't cost much more than those made of plywood and oil-based enamels.

Deconstruction and Construction

Have you ever seen an old house being bulldozed to the ground by giant claws that take out the roof, walls, windows, and doors in a few chomps? How many homes have been turned into piles of debris and hauled off to the local landfill? How many materials that could have been salvaged have instead been mixed in with toxic debris and materials that will never decompose? As more people become concerned about conservation and reuse, and learn more about the cost of building, this scenario will become less prevalent. Many cities are even starting to require that a certain percentage of building waste be recycled.

One person's trash is another person's treasure, which is why there are now companies specializing in home deconstruction rather than demolition. Teams of experienced salvagers go into your home and remove everything that is still in working or usable condition. Wood flooring and paneling, trimwork, tiles, countertops, cabinets, vanities, light fixtures, plumbing fixtures, windows, and doors can be

Wooden paneling and windows can be salvaged from another house and put to good use in an addition. With reclaimed furniture and lighting fixtures, you might end up with an entire room that was created with no new materials.

CONTRACTOR
IRIS HARRELL ON

Choosing What to Reuse

Remodels are expensive in labor alone, so it makes financial sense to think about what you can reuse. Fixtures like sinks and tubs or building materials such as large headers are almost always worth salvaging. If you have appliances that aren't as energy or water efficient as new models but they still work, donate them to a charity and get yourself new models that conserve resources."

remodel and you'll be removing existing fixtures and finish materials, make sure you find a way to salvage everything you can and recycle the rest. Rent a construction waste bin that will go to a facility that recycles everything you tear out that can't be reused in its current state. Look for contractors who recycle or reuse 90 percent of the construction waste on their projects.

Builder Jason Lear is one such contractor. "These days we have the good fortune of being able to order mixed-debris construction-recycling bins where someone else separates that pile and recycles material such as clean wood, concrete, and metal," Lear says. Reusing materials on-site can often be a boon to builders. Lear looks for wooden studs in walls that are being removed, because the boards are often dense, heavy 2-by-4s made of old-growth wood that's stronger than what you can buy new. "And you'll pay less for them than you would for new ones," he points out. "Always try to reuse what you can on a building site, but the next best thing is to get used materials from other places."

carefully removed and reused. You can even reuse framing lumber, copper pipes, and wiring. There are also organizations that hold "open houses" before a home is demolished. People off the street bring their own tools and remove anything they want, including the bricks from the walkway and the shrubs in the landscape. Plus, they pay you for the materials they haul away.

If you're thinking of tearing down your current house to rebuild on the same spot, or even if you're doing a major

TOP A green bedroom should have an organic mattress and bedding, no-VOC paint on the walls, and plenty of fresh air and sunlight.

BOTTOM LEFT During a long remodeling project, consider setting up an alternate bathroom outdoors using fixtures found at a local salvage yard. Later, use the tub as a place to wash the dog or as an interesting raised planter.

BOTTOM RIGHT Contractors appreciate working with products that don't give off fumes that can make them dizzy or cause their eyes to water. Hopefully they will suggest these eco-friendly materials to their next client, if only for self-preservation.

OPPOSITE PAGE Colorful no-VOC paint leads the eye upward. This house enjoys healthful indoor air, and the tall central stairway acts as a siphon to move hot air up and out. Operable windows above each bedroom door ensure proper air movement even when the doors are shut.

Beyond this issue, construction dust and fumes can cause allergy and asthma symptoms, so when you check contractors' references, ask past clients whether every precaution was taken to keep the indoor air quality healthful.

If you've been careful and selected nontoxic adhesives, stains, sealants, and finishes, you will need to be vigilant that the contractor uses the materials you've specified and doesn't supplement with any of his or her own. For example, you may have ordered nontoxic glue for a flooring project, but if the contractor is used to removing dried adhesive with paint thinner, he or she might run out to the truck, grab the thinner, and use it before you have a chance to object. This would be a big blow to your indoor air quality, requiring that the space be aired out for several days. So be sure to discuss nontoxic materials not just with the head contractor but also with every other worker so that your wishes are accommodated. Usually workers are happy to follow these rules, as they appreciate job sites that don't give them headaches or breathing difficulties.

Air Quality During Construction

During a home remodel, there are often large amounts of dust, air contaminants, and VOCs released. If you are staying in the house during this time, your contractors need to pay close attention to ensure that contaminants don't make their way into your living area. A good contractor will seal off the part of the house under construction, make sure ductwork vents are closed so dust isn't spread through the house, clean up the work site daily, and keep debris from outdoor activities like sanding from blowing into open windows.

Your goal should be to use only building materials with low or no VOCs and no added formaldehyde. If this isn't possible for everything, it will be even more crucial to keep work areas sealed off from living areas.

Resources

The following organizations and manufacturers can help you create your green home.

Environmental Certifications and Organizations

Built Green
www.builtgreen.net

Cradle to Cradle
www.c2ccertified.com

Energy Star
www.energystar.gov

Forest Stewardship Council
www.fscus.org

Gray-Water Systems
www.greywater.com

Greenguard
www.greenguard.org

GreenPoint Rated Program
www.builditgreen.org/
greenpoint-rated

Green Seal
www.greenseal.org

Home Energy Rating System (HERS)
www.natresnet.org

Home Ventilating Institute
www.hvi.org

Leadership in Energy and Environmental Design (LEED)
www.usgbc.org/leed

National Green Building Program
www.nahbgreen.org

U.S. Environmental Protection Agency
www.epa.gov

U.S. Green Building Council
www.usgbc.org

WaterSense
www.epa.gov/watersense

Professional Associations and Service Providers

ADA Standards for Accessible Design
www.usdoj.gov/crt/ada/adahom1.htm

American Institute of Architects
www.aia.org

American Society of Interior Designers
www.asid.org

American Society of Landscape Architects
www.asla.org

Association of Professional Landscape Designers
www.apld.com

Bau-Biologie
www.buildingbiology.net

Building Materials Reuse Association
www.buildingreuse.org

Building Solutions
www.buildingsolutions.com
Home-performance contractors

Freecycle
www.freecycle.org
Worldwide organization promoting the giving and receiving of unwanted stuff

ReStore
www.habitat.org/env/restores.aspx
Habitat for Humanity stores featuring used building supplies

Sustainable Spaces
www.sustainablespaces.com
Home-performance retrofitter

Sustainable Building Methods

AAC Structures
www.aacstructures.com

Autoclaved Aerated Concrete (AAC)
www.aacpa.org

Insulated Concrete Forms (ICFs)
www.icfhomes.com

Rammed Earth
www.rammedearthworks.com

Structural Insulated Panels (SIPs)
www.sips.org

Building Materials and Cabinetry

Columbia Forest Products
www.columbiaforestproducts.com
Makers of PureBond plywood, with no added formaldehyde

Core Casework
www.corecasework.com
Custom eco-friendly cabinetry

Kirei
www.kireiusa.com
Reclaimed agricultural fiberboard

Neil Kelly Cabinets
www.neilkellycabinets.com
Eco-friendly semicustom cabinetry

Plyboo
www.plyboo.com
Bamboo and Durapalm plywood and flooring

Sierra Pine
www.sierrapine.com
Makers of Medite II and Medex MDF, with no added formaldehyde

Spectra Décor
www.spectradecor.com
Eco-friendly, American-made cabinet hardware

3form
www.3-form.com
Manufacturer of eco-resin panels

Woodshanti
www.woodshanti.com
Eco-friendly custom cabinetry

Countertops

Buddy Rhodes Artisan Concrete
www.buddyrhodes.com
Custom DIY concrete countertops and mixes

CaesarStone
www.caesarstone.com
Quartz composite countertops

Eco-Top
www.kliptech.com/ecotop
Solid-surface countertops made of recycled paper and bamboo fiber

EnviroGLAS
www.enviroglasproducts.com
Terazzo made of recycled glass and porcelain

Fireslate
www.fireslate.com
Fiber-cement countertops

IceStone
www.icestone.biz
Recycled-glass countertops

PaperStone
www.paperstoneproducts.com
Solid-surface countertops made of recycled paper

Richlite
www.richlite.com
Paper-based solid-surface countertops

Sonoma Cast Stone
www.sonomacaststone.com
Concrete countertops and more

Squak Mountain Stone
www.tmi-online.com
Fiber-cement countertops and more

ThinkGlass
www.thinkglass.com
Glass countertops and more

Vetrazzo
www.vetrazzo.com
Countertops made of recycled glass and concrete

Windfall Lumber
www.windfalllumber.com
Countertops and flooring made of certified and reclaimed wood

Floor and Wall Coverings

AFM Safecoat
www.afmsafecoat.com
Low- and no-VOC paints, stains, sealers, and cleaners for chemically sensitive people

American Clay
www.americanclay.com
Natural-earth plaster

Bedrock Industries
www.bedrockindustries.com
Recycled-glass tiles

Capri Cork
www.capricork.com
Cork and rubber flooring

EcoTimber
www.ecotimber.com
Sustainable, no-VOC prefinished wood and bamboo flooring

Expanko
www.expanko.com
Cork and rubber flooring

Fireclay Tile
www.fireclaytile.com
Tiles made from recycled materials

FLOR
www.flor.com
Modular carpet tiles

Green Planet Paints
www.greenplanetpaints.com
Plant-based paints

Madison and Grow
www.madisonandgrow.com
Sustainable wallpaper

Marmoleum
www.forbo-flooring.com
Linoleum

Merida
www.meridameridian.com
Natural-fiber area rugs

Mod Green Pod
www.modgreenpod.com
Vinyl-free wallpaper and organic fabrics

Mythic Paint
www.mythicpaint.com
No-VOC paint

Nature's Carpet
www.naturescarpet.com
Untreated wool carpet

Oceanside Glasstile
www.glasstile.com
Recycled-glass tiles

Real Milk Paint
www.realmilkpaint.com

Restoration Timber
www.restorationtimber.com
Reclaimed-wood flooring

Roppe
www.roppe.com
Rubber floor tiles

Rubio Monocoat
www.rubiomonocoat.com
No-VOC oil-based wood finish

Sandhill Industries
www.sandhillind.com
Recycled-glass tiles

Teragren
www.teragren.com
Bamboo flooring, veneers, and more

Yolo Colorhouse
www.yolocolorhouse.com
Greenguard-certified, environmentally responsible paint with a natural palette

Furniture, Bedding, and Mattresses

Cisco Brothers
www.ciscobrothers.com
Sustainable upholstered furniture

EKLA Home
www.eklahome.com
Sustainable upholstered furniture

Loop
www.looporganic.com
Organic bed and bath linens

Naturepedic
www.naturepedic.com
Organic mattresses and accessories

Pixel Organics
www.pixelorganics.com
Organic bedding and more

Q Collection
www.qcollection.com
Sustainable furniture and fabric

Q Collection JR
www.qcollectionjunior.com
Healthful, eco-friendly nursery furniture and bedding

Raksha Bella
www.rakshabellaorganic.com
Organic bedding

Royal Pedic
www.royal-pedic.com
Organic mattresses and accessories

Savvy Rest
www.savvyrest.com
Organic mattresses and accessories

Light and Heat

EcoSmart
www.ecosmartfire.com
Freestanding eco-friendly fireplaces

Helen Bilt
www.helenbilt.com
Custom lighting fixtures made of reused materials

Lite2Go
www.knoend.com
Lite2go lamp and other eco-friendly designs

Moso Pendant
www.schmittdesign.com
Bamboo pendants

Propellor Design
www.propellor.ca
Bamboo lighting fixtures and more

Solatube
www.solatube.com
Daylighting solutions

Tulikivi
www.tulikivi.com
Soapstone fireplaces

Exterior Products

Allsop Home and Garden
www.allsopgarden.com
Solar lanterns and garden art

ELT Easy Green
www.eltgreenroofs.com
Green roof systems

GreenGrid
www.greengridroofs.com
Modular rooftop gardens

Greenroofs.com
www.greenroofs.com
Resources and information on green roof systems

Pennington Seed
www.penningtonseed.com
SmartSeed lawn requires less water

Pervious Concrete
www.perviouspavement.org

Rainwater HOG
www.rainwaterhog.com
Rainwater-collection containers

The Safe Sand Company
www.safesand.com
Silica-free sand

SIL-LEED
www.cbf11.com
Fiber-cement siding

SYNLawn
www.synlawn.com
Synthetic lawn

Trex Co.
www.trex.com
Composite decking

Whit McLeod
www.whitmcleod.com
Outdoor furniture made of recycled wood

Photography

Cover: This kitchen proves that being eco-friendly doesn't require sacrificing personal style. What looks like solid exotic-wood cabinets are actually panels made of a digital image of the real thing laminated between two sheets of glass. Later, both the bright green and wood-grain panels can be easily changed without replacing the cabinet boxes, which were constructed of no-added-formaldehyde MDF made from 100% post consumer recycled content. This flexibility prevents unnecessary remodels down the line that would produce dumpsters full of waste. The cabinets are topped with hefty concrete counters that incorporate flecks of recycled rice hulls for added sparkle. Cabinets by M8,

www.m8style.com; countertops by Concreteworks, www.concreteworks.com. Courtesy of AAC Structures: 149 bottom; Jean Allsopp and Harry Taylor/SPC: 55 left, 58; Courtesy of Paula Baker-Laporte: 4 top left; Alan K. Barley/Courtesy of Barley & Pfeiffer Architects: 190; Edmund Barr: 15 top center; Robert J. Bennett: 169 top left; Johnny Bouchier/Redcover.com: 135 middle left; Barbara Bourne: 29 bottom right, 47 top, 47 middle; Courtesy of Broan-NuTone: 102 bottom middle; Rob D. Brodman: 31 top right, 44 top right, 44 middle right, 45 top left, 57 top right, 90 middle right, 143 top left, 164 left, 172; Ed Caldwell: 156; Courtesy of Cisco Brothers: 60 top, 61; Courtesy of Clarum Homes: 149 top left, 149

top right; Construction Photography/Corbis: 9 upper right; Laurie E. Dickson: 2 left, 22 right, 27, 73 top left, 77 top, 82 left, 95 bottom, 106, 126 bottom right, 127 top, 150 middle, 152 top, 153 bottom; Ken Druse: 166 bottom; Dan Duchars/Redcover.com: 42 top; Michael Dwyer/Alamy: 155 top left; Courtesy of EcoTimber: 30, 31 bottom right, 35, 109; Courtesy of Eleek: 90 top middle; Courtesy of Matt Elliott: 5 middle left; William E. Enos, EmeraldLight Photography: 10 bottom, 75 bottom, 81 bottom, 107 middle left, 107 middle right, 114, 142; Etsa/Corbis: 22 left; Eric Evans/Corner House Stock Photo, Inc.: 173; Courtesy of Fired Earth: 86 bottom; Courtesy of Eric Corey Freed: 4 top right; William Geddes/Beateworks/

Corbis: 83 right; Tria Giovan: 31 top left, 39 left, 53 top right, 56 middle right, 155 middle; Nathan Good: 15 top right; Goodshoot/Corbis: 200 bottom right; Jay Graham: 96; John Granen: 9 bottom, 36, 37 top; Courtesy of Green Roofs for Healthy Cities (www.greenroofs.org), and Jeffrey L. Bruce & Company: 157 middle left; Courtesy of Green Roofs for Healthy Cities (www.greenroofs.org), Hoerr Schaudt Landscape Architects, LLC and Scott Shigley: 157 middle right; Tom Grill/Corbis: 153 top left; Steven Gunther: 176; Jamie Hadley: 93 middle; Courtesy of Iris Harrell: 4 bottom; Margot Hartford: 94 bottom left; Ken Hayden/Redcover.com: 48 middle, 49; Saxon Holt: 154, 157 top left, 166 top, 170, 172 middle left, 172 middle right, 174 right, 182 top; D.A. Horchner: 178 top, 179 top; Image Studios: 41 top; IPS Co., Ltd./Corbis: 121 bottom; Michael Jensen: 70; Richard Leo Johnson/Beateworks/Corbis: 121 top; Courtesy of Michelle Kaufmann: 5 top left; Courtesy of Kirei: 52 top right; Courtesy of Kliptech Composites: 90 top right; Courtesy of Knoend: 128 top right; Chuck Kuhn: 48 top, 168 top, 168 bottom, 169 bottom; Kim Kurian: 153 top right; Courtesy of Kelly LaPlante: 5 top right; Courtesy of Jason Lear: 5 middle right; David Duncan Livingston: 90 top left; Nic Lohoux: 3 center, 123; Paul Massey/Redcover.com: 23 left, 78 bottom right; E. Andrew McKinney: 125 middle left, 127 bottom; Connie Moberly/Courtesy of Barney & Pfeiffer Architects: 193 top; Daniel Nadelbach: 32 bottom left; Emily Nathan: 94 top right; John O'Hagan and Rob Lagerstrom/SPC: 53 top left; David Papazian/Beateworks/Corbis: 155 top right; Jerry Pavia: 169 top right; Frank Paul Perez/Red Lily Studios: 151; Linda Lamb Peters: 179 bottom; Courtesy of Peter Pfeiffer: 5 bottom right; Norm Plate: 177 top right; Courtesy of Plyboo: 34 top, 34 middle left, 52 bottom right; Courtesy of Q Collection: 60 bottom; Redcover.com: 13 bottom right, 108 bottom; Ken Rice: 40 gutter; Lisa Romerein: 12, 41